Image Is Everything

Image Is Everything

Marvin Winans

Treasure House

An Imprint of

Destiny Image® Publishers, Inc.
P.O. Box 310
Shippensburg, PA 17257-0310

"For where your treasure is
there will your heart be also." Matthew 6:21

ISBN 1-56043-262-4

For Worldwide Distribution
Printed in the U.S.A.

iv

Treasure House books are available through these fine distributors outside the United States:

Christian Growth, Inc.
Jalan Kilang-Timor, Singapore 0315

Omega Distributors
Ponsonby, Auckland, New Zealand

Rhema Ministries Trading
Randburg, Rep. of South Africa

Salvation Book Centre
Petaling, Jaya, Malaysia

Successful Christian Living
Capetown, Rep. of South Africa

Vine Christian Centre
Mid Glamorgan, Wales, United Kingdom

WA Buchanan Company
Geebung, Queensland, Australia

Word Alive
Niverville, Manitoba, Canada

This book and all other Destiny Image
and Treasure House books are
available at Christian bookstores everywhere.

Call for a bookstore nearest you.
1-800-722-6774
Or reach us on the Internet: **http://www.reapernet.com**

Dedication

To my mother and father, Elders David and Delores Winans; for me, you were the perfect image of what parents should be.

To my sons Mario, Marvin, Jr., and Josiah; I pray I will be God's image of a father to you.

To all my brothers and sisters.

To the wonderful ministry of which the Lord has made me undershepherd: Perfecting Church. Thanks for allowing me to share this book with the world.

To my administrator Cindy Flowers, my secretary Charlotte Y. Dunbar, and my editor Larry Walker. Thanks for your patience and help in writing this book. I never could have done it without you.

Finally, to the entire Body of Christ. May you read this book and be changed in your thinking, and may the revelation of who you are in Him come alive and make you one with His purpose.

Contents

Introduction

Growing up in America during the turbulent years of the 1960's and 1970's was quite exciting. Every time you would turn around there was a revolt of some kind or another. The winds of change were blowing, and it seemed like everyone was "anti-establishment." People were crying for freedom, and the wisdom of the day declared that anything representing uniformity had to be abolished.

Just before this wave of insurgence, America was a more predictable nation. There were internationally recognized symbols that represented her purpose and resolve. We had a clear and concise vision of what our generation, as the future of this country, should strive for. We knew what was expected of us as her burgeoning hope. The Church was still a shining beacon of guidance in those days, giving direction in the waning moments of this tumultuous era.

Today, all symbols of stability and all standards of excellence and morality have been obliterated, and our world is in desperate need of help. The only way the world will change is for the Church of the Lord Jesus to rise up in supernatural authority to assume her rightful position in society.

The business world, our social structures, our decaying educational institutions, our recreational habits, and even our health and charitable institutions desperately need to have an image placed before them. They all need a lighthouse of hope and stability shining a guiding light to help them steer a safe course through the choppy waters of our man-made storm.

This confused generation is faced with some very tough questions, such as the right to die (doctor-assisted suicide), the legalization of drugs, and same sex marriages, just to name a few. The Church cannot take a backseat and simply "drift with the tide." The Lord does not want the Church to react, but rather to act. In this atmosphere of uncertainty and desperate hunger for leadership, the Church cannot afford to say one thing while doing another. To fulfill our destiny as individuals and as a body of believers united in Christ, we must be who and what we say we are! If we are going to change the world, then we must have the image of the Father stamped in our spirits. That is why this *image is everything*!

Chapter 1

Before the Beginning, God Imagined

I was watching a sports program on television when a commercial interrupted the coverage. The product was being hawked by a famous tennis player, and at the end of the commercial a slogan resounded from the speakers and spread across the picture tube: *Image Is Everything!*

My immediate reaction was, "Image is nothing!" Since the athlete doing the pitch had not won a championship in recent memory, it seemed to prove my point that "image is nothing." Here was an athlete who brimmed with potential, yet he seemed unable to deliver. The more the station aired the ad, the more contemptible it became to me.

I held onto my opinion until one day I saw the light. I hadn't planned it or expected it, but I found myself being verbally attacked and accused of things that were not true. (There is nothing more painful than character assassination!) As I stood there in disbelief, the Spirit of God suddenly spoke out of my inner man to my would-be assassin, *"You will not make me change the image I have of myself."*

The next morning, while preparing to speak before my congregation about becoming more like Christ, I was searching for a phrase that would capture the essence of the truth God had shown me. What should the Holy Spirit bring to my mind but that previously despicable slogan: *"Image Is Everything!"*

The Greatest Culprit of All

From that day until this, I have received a continual revelation of the importance of image. Modern society suffers from many ills—all of which have contributed to the downward spiral of the standard of living. But the greatest culprit of them all is our lack of image. If a five-year-old boy does not have the image of a man or father in front of him, then more than likely, he will grow up deficient in his abilities to properly raise a family. If that same boy does not have a mother to teach him how to love his wife and show tenderness and concern to his children, he will grow up unable to share his feelings with his spouse and offspring.

There must be an image or reference in the minds of boys and girls, and of grown men and women, that sets the boundaries for what is right and wrong, normal and abnormal, correct and incorrect. Without an image, we grope aimlessly through life, reacting to our whims and desires instead of to what is true and accurate. We need an image that points us in the right direction. We need an image that says, "Do as I do, and not just as I say." We need an image because "image is everything!"

Every Workman Must First Imagine

I am certain that everyone will agree—from the artist to the architect, from the fashion designer to the cake decorator—that nothing of substantial and enduring beauty comes into being without forethought and imagination.

Every workman must first imagine the size, color, material, function, weight, and height of a thing before attempting to create a work. Although no one else can tell what he is making, he knows because he has *seen the finished product*, if only in his head. Every inventor and creator, from the potter to the painter, reserves the right to destroy and remake the piece or project until it *conforms to the image he has envisioned.*

> *The word which came to Jeremiah from the Lord, saying, Arise, and go down to the potter's house, and there I will cause thee to hear My words. Then I went down to the potter's house, and, behold, he wrought a work on the wheels. And the vessel that he made of clay was marred in the hand of the potter: so he made it again another vessel, as seemed good to the potter to make it. Then the word of the Lord came to me, saying, O house of Israel, cannot I do with you as this potter? saith the Lord. Behold, as the clay is in the potter's hand, so are ye in Mine hand, O house of Israel* (Jeremiah 18:1-6).

As was the case with Israel in the days of the prophet Jeremiah, God desired to make of Israel a nation that would reflect His majesty, glory, power, and personality. The problem with us, as finite beings, is that we are limited to what we can see or have seen. We are bound to our limitations, perceptions, and imaginations. And often, to our own hurt, we argue with God's capability to perform what He has imagined for us.

My father was employed by the Chrysler Motor Corporation during my childhood years. I remember the times he brought home books filled with futuristic car designs. Even though he brought them home in the mid-1960's, those books contained illustrations of cars that are just now being introduced in the mid-1990's! They featured turbine engines, air bags, and the aerodynamic body designs that have swept through the industry just recently.

Prototype models of the automobiles we drive today were designed and built 30 years ago, and the cars we will drive in the next millennium have already been built. If this theory holds true for every kind of invention, from cars to the wild contraptions in the inventors' garages, then how can we, with any intelligent conviction, entertain the thought that the earth is an "accident"?

Only a few miles from most "new car" dealerships you can find dealers of another kind—the salvage and junk dealers. Thousands of gutted car bodies, rusted parts, and dented and marred fenders give mute testimony to the faded glory of earlier days and purer lines.

This planet, which at the very least is 6,000 years old, with all its enduring beauty and splendor, hues, shapes, and qualities, is a masterpiece of contrast in balance. It, too, bears the marks and scars of time, including the effects of the Ice Age, catastrophic floods, volcanoes, tidal waves, and the recent ravages of man-made pollution. The shrinking ozone layer, the disappearance of tropical rain forests, and the unsettling influence of increasingly erratic weather patterns are wreaking environmental devastation. Yet I can still look out across the meadow and see the timeless brilliance of a rose. Somehow the genius of the original intent and design of the earth still shows through. Jehovah God, the "self-existing One," has left us enough clues about Himself for us to draw some accurate conclusions for some obvious questions.

Regardless of the weather or the political whims of mankind, we can, with undaunted accuracy, forecast the rising of the sun out of the east and its setting in the west. How can we then say that all this was left to chance and spontaneity? What kind of intellectual suicide is required for an "educated person" to say the universe "just evolved" without "someone" first imagining it?! Based on this unquestionable circumstantial evidence, I must declare that *"before the beginning, God imagined."*

The first verse of the Book of Genesis declares, "In the beginning God created the heaven and the earth." *Genesis* is a Greek word meaning "origin, source, generation, or beginning." The original Hebrew title is *Bereishit,* which means "in the beginning."

It is not my desire to give you a course in etymology, but we need to understand the origin of the word to grasp the meaning of the phrase. In the original text, the Hebrew word for beginning is *reshiyth*, which means "the first, in place, in time, in order or rank."[1] Here it is made clear that this is the first earth and the first heaven that God ever created. The fact that there is no record of any other creation before this one will prove vital as it relates to salvation and the redemption of mankind.

The second verse reads, "And the earth was without form, and void; and darkness was upon the face of the deep" (Gen. 1:2a). Since we know that God is the Father of lights, and that in Him is no darkness at all (Jas. 1:17; 1 Jn. 1:5), could it be that God has allowed the writer to take us into the darkroom of His own imagination? How many times have you and I closed our eyes in utter darkness to gain a better perception of what it was we were imagining?

The Creative Force of God

The Bible reveals that the word of God was a creative force from the beginning. "And God said, Let there be light: and there was light" (Gen. 1:3). The Book of Hebrews confirms the creative power of God's word: "Through faith we understand that the worlds *were framed by the word of God*, so that things which are seen were not made of things which do appear" (Heb. 11:3).

Jesus *spoke the word* and the centurion's servant was healed. He spoke and the stormy sea became calmed. He spoke a word and demons fled from the demoniac of the Gadarenes. At a word, leprosy was driven from contorted bodies, and the dead rose to stand before Him! God's word is a creative force.

When I was a little boy, my grandmother would often admonish me, "Boy, think before you speak!" Can we say any less of God? This has the ring of divine truth. The *thoughts* of God precede His word and are a creative force in their own right! God said, "Surely as I have *thought*, so shall it come to pass" (Is. 14:24b). God first thinks or imagines a thing in His mind, then He creates it after His own purpose. This is an important principle as you shall see in chapters to come.

One of my favorite Scriptures is found in the Book of Jeremiah: "For I know the thoughts that I think toward you, saith the Lord, thoughts of peace, and not of evil, to give you an expected end" (Jer. 29:11). The word for "expected" in the Hebrew is *tiqvah*. It literally means "a cord," and refers to "the thing that I long for."[2] There is an "attachment" connecting what God *thinks* to what God *does*. God's actions are not independent of His thoughts. What are you thinking right now? (A deed is not far behind...)

The Hebrew word for "thought" is *machasbebeth,* and one of its meanings is "imagination."[3] What the Lord is declaring is most sweet and wonderful! In essence He is saying, "I know what I have imagined about you, and not only am I able to imagine, but I am also able to bring it to pass."

If God's imagination is perfect, and His ability to bring it into being is unshaken, then why is His highest creation so flawed, so selfish, and so saturated with sin? The problem has to do with the departure of the creation from the pattern of the Creator's imagination.

> *And God said, Let Us make man in Our image, after Our likeness: and let them have dominion…. So God created man in His own image, in the image of God created He him; male and female created He them* (Genesis 1:26-27).

Image is everything. What is God's image? The Book of Genesis clearly states the "blueprint" of our origin. The Hebrew word for "image" is *tselem,* which means "to shade, a phantom; or figuratively, resemblance…a representative figure."[4] It refers to an exact copy—you have been stamped out of the Original. If we were created in the image of God, then this totally nullifies the myth based on the theory of evolution that says man descended from monkeys. If we did evolve from apes, then what does our future hold?

Endnotes

1. James Strong, *Strong's Exhaustive Concordance of the Bible* (Peabody, MA: Hendrickson Publishers, n.d.), #7225 (Hebrew). These meanings also come from their prime root words and so may not be exact to *Strong's*.

2. *Strong's*, #6960 (Hebrew).

3. *Strong's*, #4284 (Hebrew).

4. *Strong's*, #6754 (Hebrew).

Chapter 2

The Image Stealer

At the close of Chapter 1, we found ourselves challenging the theory of the descent of man from "lower primates." This point is particularly important to you and I because "*a thief cannot steal what you do not have*." Satan stole something from Adam and Eve, and it was more than just a paradise lost.

One of the members of the church I pastor is an insurance claims adjuster. From time to time, she'll tell me interesting stories. Some of the stories she tells are quite funny, and some are unbelievable. She says that in the U.S. alone, thousands of people submit fraudulent theft claims every month. When insurance company representatives arrive, these people come up with lists of "possessions" they *have never owned* that have been "lost" in a theft.

"My four-head VCR is gone, and so is my new 48-inch wide-screen TV!" Others exclaim, "My five-carat diamond ring was stolen!" When the agent asks, "Do you have the sales receipts, cancelled checks, or credit card records to verify these purchases?" they suddenly start backpedaling to cover their deception. Although there may have been a legitimate claim, a burglary of some sort, because they tacked on things that they never owned, the whole claim was fraudulent and puts them at risk for criminal prosecution. Why? Because a thief cannot steal what you do not have! Everyone knows a thief can only steal what you already have.

"And God said, Let Us make man [male and female] in *Our image*, after *Our likeness*" (Gen. 1:26a). Through the chicanery of the enemy, Adam and Eve lost sight of *their image*. Mankind possessed paradise and immortality as God's handcrafted representatives formed from the earth but inspired and stamped from His own eternal substance and in His image. Yet, we pawned it off for the ethereal hope of godlike wisdom, only to receive the dark and weighty knowledge of sin and its inevitable wage of death. The thief stole the best we had and left us with a distorted image of who we are.

> *For as* [a man] *thinketh in his heart, so is he* (Proverbs 23:7a).

During the time my mother-in-law was staying in our home, the Lord graciously healed her of diabetes. She had been giving herself insulin injections, until the day she had an open vision and saw Jesus. The Lord told her, "I am able to give you power over that needle." She acted on that word by faith and stopped the insulin injections without having any reaction. Before that time, any slight deviation from her medication schedule would trigger dangerous reactions. She enjoyed symptom-free health for many weeks. Then she went back to the doctor for her regular visit, fully expecting to hear him say her blood sugar was normal. To her disappointment he told her, "The sugar level is still high."

After hearing this several times, she reluctantly resumed her insulin injections, and her sensitivity to the slightest deviation in medication returned—along with a crushing sense of failure. She said, "I don't understand it. I *know* God healed me." Finally, I told her from the pulpit one Sunday, "The Lord says you need to understand something. Just because you proclaim healing, and just because God does heal you, this does not mean that the thief will not come back *to take what God has given you!*"

When you say, "I am healed," in a sense you have given a signal to the thief that you have a new possession worth stealing. (Remember, he can only take what you have.) God wants you to know that the enemy wants to rob you of one thing more than your house, your land, and all your possessions and money put together! The devil wants to steal your image. He wants to rob you of *the knowledge of who you are!*

In the beginning, God gave man (male and female) *dominion* over everything in the garden. As long as the man and woman kept the image their Creator had given them, their authority and identities were impregnable. The devil said to himself, "I can't quite get to them as long as they walk together." The Scriptures declare, "Two are better than one..." (Eccl. 4:9). So he decided to target the woman alone.

The deceiver had one goal: to change the image she had of herself. He knew that was the only way to disrupt the peace of paradise.

> As long as you see yourself as God sees you...
> As long as you walk in the authority that you were created to walk in...
> As long as you know who you are...
> ...the devil is in trouble.

Satan must have hissed to himself, "If I can only twist the woman's image, then her influence might distort Adam's self-perception as well." So he walked up to the woman and said:

> *...Yea, hath God said, Ye shall not eat of every tree of the garden? And the woman said unto the serpent, We may eat of the fruit of the trees of the garden: but of the fruit of the tree which is in the midst of the garden, God hath said, Ye shall not eat of it, neither shall ye touch it, lest ye die. And the serpent said unto the woman, Ye shall not surely die: for God doth know that in the day ye eat thereof, then your eyes shall be opened, and ye shall be as gods, knowing good and evil* (Genesis 3:1-5).

The enemy said: "Ye shall *not* surely die." (Now I am still trying to find out the difference between "die" and "*surely* die." I have always believed that you are either dead or you aren't.) The devil had already experienced the closest thing to death that had ever existed in the spirit realm when he was forcibly removed from God's presence and stripped of his celestial glory in shame. He knew the woman God made wouldn't fall over dead the second she bit into the forbidden fruit, so he played word games to make her question God's integrity.

The devil knew that if he could get Eve to doubt *part* of God's word, it would weaken her confidence in the rest of His words, and force her to *change her image* of God. He's still hissing the same lie today, but with different words, "Well, that isn't what God *really means* there. Now you and I know that a loving God could never really send anybody to hell...."

Satan told the woman, "For God doth know...your eyes shall be opened, and ye shall be as gods..." (Gen. 3:5). God fashioned this woman from Adam's rib and breathed into her the same thing that is in Adam—which was Himself (God). The devil didn't want this woman to see who she really was! "I have to make her think that she is 'not all that.' If I get her to believe that she really isn't much more than a second-rate creature, then I'll get her to strive for something that she doesn't really need!"

"I have to shift her attention away from God's image," the devil thought. "I can't have these creatures walking around here like they are the salt of the earth with the power of dominion. Oh no, I have to change their image of themselves." He decided to create a scenario that would plant seeds of doubt and desire in the woman's mind.

When you doubt who you are,
your enemy can deceive you.

"Woman," the devil said, "God knows that if you eat of this tree, you are going to be like Him." Every time I read Genesis chapter 3, I want to shout to Eve, "But Eve, you are *already* like God! He made you that way." Unfortunately, Adam either wasn't able or willing to tell his wife this, and she bought the devil's lie and distorted her image of God forever.

Can you imagine this woman's existence with Adam in paradise up until that moment? She was surrounded by gentle, submissive animals, most or all of which could talk, sing, or squawk intelligently (remember, the devil used a walking snake to fulfill his purposes). She and Adam had everything under control in paradise. Adam and Eve didn't even have arguments because they exercised dominion together in perfect harmony, as two halves joined together as one. This picture of peace changed into a fractured existence of separation, struggle, and anxiety once Adam allowed the devil to tell Eve that *she was not all that she thought she was.* Although the words of God are a creative force, the negative lies and insinuations of devils and men are destructive.

The devil made the first woman believe there was something missing in her life. She began to suspect there was something God was "holding back" from her because He was afraid to give her "equal status" with Himself. (This is the same iniquity that transformed Lucifer, the archangel of light, into satan, the fallen angel—the adversary and enemy of our souls.)

The devil is still lying to mankind today. He is trying to disturb the peace you have and steal the image you have received from the hand of God. Once the first woman bought satan's lie, everything changed. Now the same fruit that she had walked past countless times (without even noticing or touching it) suddenly began to pull on her.

The fruit hadn't changed. God hadn't changed. The problem was in the woman's image. This woman was *surrounded* by fruit. The last thing she wanted or needed was another piece of fruit. Yet, satan's lie and her loss of self-esteem made her desire what formerly went unnoticed. The forbidden fruit had made her see herself differently.

The devil sells all his inventory the same way. He creates a sense of lack, loss, or lust for "something we don't have" by making us think we are not complete until we experience or consume his wares. Every day, drug dealers on our street corners and in our schools convince thousands of youngsters that they are "missing out on something." They say, "You haven't experienced life; you don't know what it is about. You need to get high to really enjoy yourself. Everybody's doing it, and how could they *all* be wrong? You're the only one left on the sidelines here." Suddenly, what never used to bother these kids becomes inviting and almost irresistible. Why? *They have allowed the words of others to change the image they have of themselves.*

When Eve turned her gaze from the serpent to the tree, what was once forbidden suddenly became desirous *because she had received and believed the devil's devious lie.* Now her thinking patterns began to follow the twisted route of rebellion. "Somehow this tree is going to make me wise," she must have imagined. "The fruit of this tree will make me *better than I am* if I disobey God just this once."

When the woman plucked and ate the forbidden fruit, she instantly shared her find with her willing husband (who knew better). Their eyes were suddenly opened to the possibility and existence of evil (see Gen. 3:6-7). They now experienced firsthand the pain and separation caused by disobedience to the plan, purposes, and pronouncements of God. In that instant, the covering glory of God lifted from their bodies. In one awful moment, they saw and experienced the shame caused by sin. It was in this moment that they saw they were "naked."

Nakedness is meaningless when you have nothing to conceal. Once you have something to hide, however, nakedness is embarrassing. Adam and Eve were unclothed from the moment they were made to the day they tried to fashion coverings from fig leaves. Genesis 2:25 says that in the beginning, they were both naked and were not ashamed. It was after they disobeyed the word of God that their image of themselves changed. Now they felt compelled to hide from one another: "Adam, I just can't see you the way I used to see you." So Adam began to hide from Eve, and Eve ran from Adam. Then they both ran from God in *fear:* "And [Adam] said, I heard Thy voice in the garden, and I was afraid, because I was naked; and I hid myself" (Gen. 3:10).

What had changed? God used to meet Adam and Eve each day for a cool walk through the garden and a time of sweet communion between the created and the Creator.

Adam and Eve would normally run to meet God whenever they heard Him walking in the garden, but something tragic had happened.

When Adam and Eve lost sight of who they were, they no longer welcomed the presence of God. They fled from His presence because they saw themselves differently. Their nakedness was laid bare in the absence of God's glory. Overwhelmed by their new knowledge of sin and shame, the very thought of encountering God in their spiritual nakedness was suddenly frightening. The same God who had pesonally made them had somehow become someone to fear and avoid, rather than someone they would run to meet.

When Adam and Eve hid themselves in the trees of the garden, their actions displayed their sin more graphically than an open confession. Only the shame of sin could drive them to hide from God behind aprons of fig leaves and the tree trunks of paradise. God knew all this when He cried out, "Adam, where art thou?" (see Gen. 3:9)

Adam responded from the "safety" of the trees, "God, we were naked so we hid ourselves from You." Notice what God says: *"Who told thee that thou wast naked?"* (Gen. 3:11) God already knew the answers to His questions, but He wanted Adam to tell Him the truth from his own mouth.

"Where did you get that from? I never told you that. I never told you that you needed to hide from Me! Where did you get that perception? When did you see yourself as naked? I clothed you," God was saying. "You were just and righteous as far as I was concerned, because I clothed you with something invisible, I gave you something that the world couldn't see. Who told you that you were naked, Adam? I didn't tell you that you were inadequate. I didn't tell you that you were insufficient. I didn't tell you that you don't have what it takes. Who gave you that distorted view and image?"

Right away, Adam "covered himself" with yet another excuse: "The woman *whom Thou gavest* to be with me, *she* gave me of the tree, and I did eat" (Gen. 3:12). "Well, it was 'that woman' that You gave me. She changed my perception of myself. She distorted the image I have of myself." I want you to know, mister, that you haven't been validated until a woman validates you.

Any time a woman tells you that "you ain't nothing," then her words will go right down through your bones! You may act like a macho man and say it doesn't hurt, but you will go home and cry when you're all alone. Any time a woman tells a man, "You're not a man!" her words become a sword that will tear him up inside. Adam, the first ruler of the earth, the man who received the power of dominion directly from God, suddenly felt inadequate. "That woman You gave me caused me to change the image I have of myself."

"Eve, who told you?" The woman quickly pointed her finger to avoid the blame. "That serpent did it. He changed the image I had of myself and deceived me into eating the fruit." God knew things had changed. Why? Because the devil succeeded in changing the way Adam and Eve saw themselves. *Image is everything!*

Satan was determined to change Eve's image of herself because it was the *only way* he could plant evil in the heart of mankind in paradise! "Eve, I want you to eat this fruit because it will make you like a god. God doesn't want you to eat it because He knows it will make you like Him." That temptation should not have worked for the same reason it shouldn't work today—they were already created like Him. *When we fail to see who we are, then we open the door for deception.*

If satan can change the image you have of yourself, he can change the image that you have of your God.

If we ever really understand what it means to be created in the image and likeness of God, then we will know we are *important and special!* We have been handcrafted to display the character and nature of God Himself on this earth! We should move and behave like God, because our *image* should be like *His image!*

Do you really believe that you were created in the image and likeness of God? He is great, omniscient, and omnipotent. If you were really created in His image, then you were created with genuine dominion and power! We have divine authority as delegated representatives and exact copies stamped from His substance and nature! You and I have the privilege and opportunity to change things in God's name.

As in the days of Adam and Eve, God has placed us in the earth and breathed His life and substance into us for a very specific purpose. Only this time around, as the reborn sons of Adam and daughters of Eve, we are commissioned to rebuild God's garden paradise anew. We have been given dominion again. We have the ability to change things built into our image and likeness.

Does that seem like "too much power"? Why did God give us so much authority? After all, doesn't the Bible say, "What is man, that Thou art mindful of him?" Yes, but read the rest of the verse:

What is man, that Thou art mindful of him? and the son of man, that Thou visitest him? For Thou hast made him a little lower than the angels, and hast crowned him with glory and honour. Thou madest him to have dominion over the works of Thy hands: Thou hast put all things under his feet (Psalm 8:4-6).

God not only gave us authority to rule over and subdue the earth, but He also gave us supernatural authority over spiritual principalities and powers in the heavenlies! Angels are spirit beings, with certain physical attributes that certainly give them more power than humans. It only takes one angel to destroy the mightiest armies of men. Yet even though mankind was made "a little lower" than the angels, God has chosen to crown us with the *same image and authority* that He has!

So we not only have dominion over the earth, but we also have authority over any principality or power that enters our realm. The record of God's Word is indisputable: God has given us the authority to have dominion and to rule over and subdue everything in the earth. There is nothing you face that you cannot subdue. There is no challenge that you cannot subdue. We can overcome everything that we encounter—*the problem is that we don't.*

My mother and father are the proud parents of ten children, seven of which are boys. All of us have characteristics like our father. In fact, Mama could say to any one of us at any given time, "Boy, you act just like your daddy!" Now who else are we to act like?

We come into this world in the image of Adam, the first man. We look, act, and sin just like our daddy, the first Adam! Even when we know better, we still act like our daddy when we try to handle things on our own and reject the wisdom of God.

All mankind has a "daddy" problem that goes all the way back to the garden. Paul writes in Romans 1:19-23:

*Because that which may be known of God is manifest in them; for God hath shewed it unto them. For the invisible things of Him from the creation of the world are clearly seen, being understood by the things that are made, even His eternal power and Godhead; so that they are without excuse: because that, when they knew God, they glorified Him not as God, neither were thankful; but became vain in their **imaginations**, and their foolish heart was darkened. Professing themselves to be wise, they became fools, and **changed the glory of the uncorruptible God into an image made like to corruptible man**, and to birds, and fourfooted beasts, and creeping things* (Romans 1:19-23).

Once we choose to cling to our sin—even though we know better—we are forced to change the image of God in order to feel comfortable in our sin and to match our own corrupted image. But we must always remember what God told Moses in Leviticus 11:45: "...be holy, for *I am holy*." No matter how rank or unrighteous we become, we must never change the image of a holy God!

The thief can't steal what you don't possess. Yet the devil has devoted all his attention to stealing something from you and me. He wants to steal, distort, or change our most valuable possession and heritage: the image and the likeness of God. When he can get you to see yourself as a victim, your God becomes a victim. When you see yourself as a prisoner, your God becomes a prisoner. When you see yourself as sick and weakly, then your God reflects that impotent condition. That's the image that the devil wants you to have of yourself. He calls you a "lifer" in bondage. "Why, you're nothing more than a lifetime alcoholic. You are just a lifetime drug addict. Why don't you give up? You are just a lifetime abuser, and you'll always be an abuser."

The devil wants to make your "lifelong" addiction pass on from generation to generation, just as the sin nature has come to you all the way from Adam. The good news is that once you find out who you are in God, all that nonsense stops, because there is nothing you cannot overcome and subdue when you walk in His image! What you need is a clear view of who God is. If you ever get a clear view of who God is, then you will get a clear view of who you are!

Chapter 3

You Can't Get Away From You!

God first revealed the "law of sowing and reaping" when He created the natural world and every living thing to reproduce "after its own kind" (see Gen. 1:21,24-25). That is why no human being has a "say-so" about how he is born.

God formed Adam's body using the rich soil of the garden He had made, and He breathed life into Adam from His own substance and nature. His design was perfect, and His pleasure in mankind was complete. He created mankind, male and female, to reproduce *after their own kind* in untainted perfection. Before the first natural conception, however, Adam and Eve's act of disobedience "sowed" the spiritual seed of sin and death into their lives and bodies. That seed produced a deadly harvest of which you and I are a part. Their offspring from that day to this have been born "after their own kind" with the terminal disease of sin and death!

> *Wherefore, as by one man sin entered into the world, and death by sin; and so death passed upon all men, for that all have sinned: ... Nevertheless death reigned from Adam to Moses, even over them that had not sinned after the similitude of Adam's transgression, who is the figure of Him that was to come* (Romans 5:12,14).

Our movie theaters are regularly filled with movies about "cyborgs" (half-human, half-electronic beings) and "supermutants" with superhuman powers and abilities. My advice to you is to not get carried away with these earthbound imaginations—they are just fiction. I realize the possibilities and realities of cell mutations causing physical abnormalities and handicaps. The truth still remains, for the most part, that most humans enter this life through the normal birth process. Most human offspring are born with two eyes located in the front of the head, with two ears on the side of the head, and so forth.

My point is simply this: No one can say before their conception or birth, "Well, I think I want my arm in the back" or "I want the brain of an Einstein, the talent of a Michelangelo, and the body of an Olympic athlete." You were pretty much born in the same way and with the same characteristics as the people who were born before you. We just weren't given the privilege of "self-selection."

Your genetic makeup determines the color of your skin, eyes, and hair. Everything about you in the natural deals with the seed. In fact, your father's seed even determined your gender! In the Dark Ages, common men and kings alike blamed their wives if they did not bear them sons to carry on their names and lineage. Thanks to modern science, we now know that gender is determined solely by the seed of the male! Brother, it is not your wife's fault if you're not having the little girl or boy you "ordered."

The law of sowing and reaping isn't restricted to the natural realm of human reproduction or nature. It is even more important in the realm of the spirit. What is God trying to say to us in our spirits? If we're going to do what we have heard, if we're going to accomplish what God has called us to accomplish, then we must understand where we come from. We must understand where we get the right to do what we are called to do. What empowers you to say what you say, or to live like you live? God declares that the beginning and the destiny of a child is in its seed.

Genetic studies are in progress today that will tell you at birth what the life expectancy is for your child! Scientists are working to reach the point where they can tell you at the moment of birth, "This child, barring accidents, is going to live to be 60. And this one should live to be 80." Not only will doctors tell you how long the child is going to live, but they will also tell you the diseases they are most likely to contract, such as cancer, heart disease, arthritis, etc. This may seem impossible, but it's true. The medical profession won't be making these statements based on mere guesswork. They will base their statements on the information they gather directly from each baby's family medical history!

We just can't escape the fact that God made every living thing to reproduce "after its own kind." If your mama was born black and beautiful, then there is no sense in your bleaching your hair and skin into oblivion to look white. Likewise, if you are Caucasian, stop risking skin cancer just to get *darker*. I tell people, "Just get happy with your color and your skin pigmentation. Get happy with your hair and body form—there's nothing you can do other than keep up your general maintenance."

We reproduce ourselves in other ways, too. If we see ourselves as failures, then we will reproduce failures in our children. Research has shown that victims of child abuse tend to grow up and become child abusers themselves. The same is true of parents who are alcoholics. Their children seem to be much more likely to become alcoholics than the children of non-alcoholic parents. Sex offenders of all kinds also tend to see their behaviors reproduced in their off-spring in later years.

Now I am well aware of the power and benefits of God's Word, of faith, and of physical discipline in the care and improvement of our health and longevity. My point concerns the natural and spiritual inheritance we received from Adam and Eve through our parents.

> *The first man is of the earth, **earthy**: the second man is the Lord from heaven. As is the earthy, **such are they also that are earthy** [you and me before Christ]: and as is the heavenly, such are they also that are heavenly. And as we have borne [carried] the image of the earthy, we*

shall also bear the image of the heavenly (1 Corinthians 15:47-49).

The Bible says the first Adam was "earthy." This is translated from the Greek word *choikos*, which means "dust or dirty."[1] It comes from *choos*, which means "to heap, an earth heap."[2] It refers to loose dirt.

God is saying that He just grabbed some loose dirt and put it together to form Adam. No matter how "cute" our "dirt" is, it's still just dirt. No matter how much money you spend on dirt, it's still dirt! David declared in Psalm 39:4-5, "...that I may know how frail I am...verily every man at his best state is altogether vanity." Contrast this "nothingness" of man with the awesomeness of God and His ability to take nothing and make something out of it. David exclaims in Psalm 139:14, "I will praise Thee; for I am fearfully and wonderfully made...."

When the Bible describes the making of Adam, it is clear that his body was made in physical perfection, but without life—he could not move, perceive, or communicate—*until God breathed*! However, when God breathed His life into the first human form, that heap of loose dirt became a living soul made in the image and likeness of God.

Marvel not that I said unto thee, Ye must be born again. The wind bloweth where it listeth, and thou hearest the sound thereof, but canst not tell whence it cometh, and whither it goeth: so is every one that is born of the Spirit (John 3:7-8).

It is the breath of God that gives us His likeness. It is the Spirit of God that gives us relations with Him—not the *flesh*. This is the message that Jesus delivered to Nicodemus and is delivering to us today: "That which is born of the flesh is flesh; and that which is born of the Spirit is spirit" (Jn. 3:6). Paul confirms this in Romans 8:9b: "Now if any man have not the Spirit of Christ, he is none of His." Romans 8:14 says, "For as many as are led by the Spirit of God, they are the sons of God."

Now if you are honest, then you have to admit that your life did not have any worth *until God breathed*. You must admit that before Jesus breathed the Holy Ghost into your spirit, although you were alive, life didn't have any meaning or purpose.

A lot of people have asked me how folk get so messed up in this life. How did we get from "point A" in paradise to "point B" in perdition? The answer is simple: We do the same thing our first mama and daddy did. We don't obey the truth we have received from God.

> *Because that, when they knew God, they glorified Him not as God, neither were thankful; but became vain in their **imaginations**, and their foolish heart was darkened. Professing themselves to be wise, they became fools, and changed the glory of the uncorruptible God **into an image made like to corruptible man**...* (Romans 1:21-23).

The only way for you to be comfortable in false doctrine or to embrace a false spirit is for you to *change the image of God* into a god that you imagine is like you. Once you have been exposed to light and truth, you have to cover up your understanding to be comfortable in darkness. You have to say, "Oh, that truth isn't really necessary." You have to change the image of God into a god who is "not exactly" or altogether holy.

Paul tells us in the passage in Romans that men validate their claims by professing themselves to be wise, and they actually become fools because they try to change the image of God into their own image. It is wrong and dangerous to "explain away or justify" sin. It is better, by far, to just confess it. The Book of Proverbs says, "He that covereth his sins shall not prosper: but whoso confesseth and forsaketh them shall have mercy" (Prov. 28:13). John told us to confess our sin and leave the justification to God (see 1 Jn. 1:9).

I keep telling folks, "Stay on the right side of God. Don't try to bring Him down to your level. I don't care how long you've been in church or involved in religious activities— keep God up and out of your earthy appetites, vices, and disobedience. If you decide to turn away from the holiness of God and go back to the weak and beggarly elements, if you decide to return to those things you were delivered from— that decision is yours! *Just leave God out of it.* Don't try to change an incorruptible and holy God into a corruptible and unholy man."

When men try to justify the evil they do, they must somehow gain the understanding and acceptance of their god in order for this attempt at justification to be successful.

This is what happens every time you say, "I'm bound to this drug habit. I'm bound to alcohol. I can't conquer my craving for nicotine. I can't help my lust and my craving for sex. I can't stop the abusive behavior." Behind each of these statements is an open admission that "the god I serve is not able to deliver me—this problem or circumstance is bigger than my god; it is something that he cannot change."

Even the devil knows that *image is everything*. That is why he focuses so much of his attention on changing our image. His favorite tactic is to find an area of failure or shame in our lives that he can use with his most powerful lie: "You are a 'lifer.' There is no escape for you—this weakness, this shame will follow you the rest of your days. Just learn to live with it."

The best secular rehabilitation programs, called "Twelve Step" programs, stop short of God's best and perpetuate the devil's lie. Although they incorporate the biblical principle of honest confession of sin or addiction, along with personal accountability, they stop short of acknowledging man's need of Jesus Christ by talking only of a "Higher Power." Then they turn around and urge alcoholics, drug users, and abusers to repeat their confession every day: "I am a lifetime alcoholic. I am a drug addict. I am a lifetime abuser." This amounts to a curse that can spread from generation to generation! Although these programs bring some relief and assistance, they really offer no true cure because they do not lead people to Jesus Christ and the transforming power of the Holy Spirit.

The truth is that once you find out who you are in God, you will realize that all addictive behavior is an unnecessary evil. Why? *There is nothing that God cannot overcome!* There is nothing that God cannot subdue when you walk in His image.

Not only will God deliver you from your bondage, but He will remove from you the stigma it left behind. God tells Joshua, "This day have I rolled away the reproach of Egypt from off you" (Josh. 5:9b). You can be associated with something so long that you are identified with it. But the grace and power of God is so wonderful that it will roll the residue of bondage off you. He will change your image! He will give you a new identification.

I don't care how tainted your family history is. "Therefore if any man be in Christ, he is a new creature" (2 Cor. 5:17a). I was invited to speak at a church in a southern state that was a little different from any church in which I had previously been invited to speak. They were very friendly, but their beliefs leaned toward humanism. I asked the Lord before the service, "What should I preach?" He said, "I will give you the words to say." That is exactly what He did.

At the beginning of the service, the people were hugging themselves and loving themselves, saying, "I am wonderful and I am great." I thought, "Well, there isn't anything wrong with that, because they were made in the image of a wonderful and great God." Then the Spirit spoke to me and said, "It is all right to hug yourself *after you've been regenerated.* But it's very dangerous and deceptive to fall in love with the unregenerated man."

Whether you like it or not, whether you were born black or white, Hispanic or Oriental, you were born of Adam and, by nature, are heirs to a large and inescapable family inheritance. We are the uncontested heirs of sin, guilt, grand ingratitude, and death—the bequest of lost innocence, the patrimony of misery left behind by our fallen father, Adam. Ever since the Fall, man has made an attempt to cover up his shortcomings. The fig leaves that Adam and Eve used represent man's effort (in the absence of God) to make things better. It is no different today.

Every aspect of modern society seems to be devoted to "covering our nakedness." Daytime television programs are regularly swept by a flood of "makeover" shows where people are given new hairstyles, designer clothing, nails, and make-up—all to make the individuals feel better about themselves. The tragedy of these programs is that these people walk off the soundstages of those programs carrying the same problems they brought in with them. The advertising industry is driven to convince you that somehow their product will make you complete. "You won't be complete until you buy..." and "You can be as pretty as this famous glamour model if you use this exclusive makeup!" or "No one will really like you until you drive up in this incredibly expensive car..."

American consumers are driven like lemmings to the cliff of financial disaster with every passing fad and fancy that sweeps the fashion industry. No sooner do we shed our double-breasted suits for single-breasted suits with no-cuff trousers than we suddenly learn that double-breasted versions are back in, but with just enough changes to make our closet full of old suits totally out of style. Ladies have entire closets filled with low-hem dresses, high-hem skirts, summer "flats," dress spike heels, scarves, hats, ruffled blouses, no-sleeve blouses, jean skirts, and silk skirts. There is no end in sight, because there is no satisfaction or enduring *image* in sight!

God doesn't want you to cover up what you are. He wants you to *discover* who you are! Jacob, the second son of Isaac, is the classic example of a man who ran blindly to cover up *what* he was instead of allowing God to show him *who* he was.

Jacob stole his elder brother's birthright feeling the necessity to be the eldest, the first, and the best, in order to be accepted. After deceiving his father and stealing his brother's birthright and blessing, he ran for his life from Esau's avenging anger. He lived in fear in another country for more than 20 years. He was returning home with his wives, his sons, and his many possessions when he heard that Esau was coming with an armed troop to meet him. He sent his two wives, his family, and all his riches ahead of him in two groups to keep Esau from taking everything he had. Then he sent his servants ahead to meet Esau with gifts while he remained behind in fear.

Many years had passed since Jacob had seen his brother, Esau. But things really hadn't changed inside him. In his terror, he began to seek the God of his father, Isaac. God answered his prayer by sending an angel to meet him there.

And Jacob was left alone; and there wrestled a man with him until the breaking of the day. And when he saw that *he prevailed not against him, he touched the hollow of his thigh; and the hollow of Jacob's thigh was out of joint, as he wrestled with him. And he said, Let me go, for the day breaketh. And he said, **I will not let thee go, except thou bless me**. And he said unto him, What is thy name? And he said, Jacob. And he said, Thy name shall be called no more Jacob, but Israel: for as a prince hast thou power with God and with men, and hast prevailed* (Genesis 32:24-28).

After Jacob and the angel had wrestled all night long, the angel told Jacob to release him before daybreak, but Jacob answered very clearly, "I will not let thee go, except thou bless me." Then the angel does something very strange. Even though Jacob had asked for a blessing, the angel asked Jacob, "What is your name?" Now that is strange.

Jacob must have thought, " 'What is your name?' Well, angel, I don't know if you heard me. I told you I need a blessing. My brother is coming to kill me and you decide to ask me for my name!" When Isaac's youngest son answered, "My name is Jacob," the angel had pinpointed his problem. Jacob (*Ya'acob*) means heel-catcher, supplanter, trickster, or deceiver. All his life, Jacob had to hear his family and friends, and even his father, tear him down every time they called his name: "Hey Deceiver! Yeah, I'm talking to you, Trickster! Where are you going, Supplanter?"

Perhaps you know how Jacob felt because all your life, you've had people tell you that you are no good, that you will never be anything. "You are never going to amount to much and you are never going to do much."

If you have struggled with this kind of turmoil inside you, then God wants to deliver you like He delivered Jacob. The problem is that He can't *because you don't know who you are*. You probably realize by now that no "quick fix" or self-help solutions will do—you need a permanent change of identity and direction, and that can only happen when God puts you in touch with yourself.

We keep mistaking the symptoms for the disease. We think the problem is that we don't have enough income for our bills. We think the problem is that we don't have a husband or a wife; or the spouse we have just doesn't treat us right. We think the problem is that we didn't get that promotion. We blame all our problems on our "haves" or "have nots," but the real problem is that *we don't know who we are!*

The angel said, "Your name isn't Jacob. That's what everyone has been calling you because Jacob is *what you are* and not *who you are!* That is only what people have been expecting of you. Your name isn't Jacob—that is just what folks have become accustomed to. Your name is not Jacob; your name is Israel! The name God has given you means 'power with God.' Your name means *ruler*, because *that is who you are*. You are a ruler." Now Isaac's youngest son had to change his perception and image of himself!

The real blessing of God occurs when we change our perception of ourselves to match the image God has ordained for us! God said in the beginning, "Let Us make man [male and female] in *Our image*, after *Our likeness*" (Gen. 1:26a). The Book of Hebrews declares that Jesus, "Who being the brightness of His glory, and the *express image* of His person, and upholding all things by the word of His power, when He had by Himself purged our sins, sat down on the right hand of the Majesty on high" (Heb. 1:3).

Jesus is our example, the author and finisher of our faith (see Heb. 12:2). The Bible says you and I are destined to be "conformed" to His image (see Rom. 8:29). The image of Jesus is the "express image," the exact image of God. The Greek word for "image" is *charakter*, which means "the instrument used for engraving or carving, the mark stamped upon that instrument or wrought out on it; hence, a mark or figure burned in (Lev. 13:28) or stamped on, an impression; the exact expression (the image) of any person or thing, marked likeness, precise reproduction in every respect, i.e. facsimile."[3]

It is true that you "can't get away from you," but God wants to change your perception of "you" to match your image in Christ. As long as you see yourself as God sees you, walk in the authority He has given you, and hold to your identity as God's representative, created in God's image, *then you will fulfill your purpose with joy*! Every day will be a great one. We have carried around all the bad things people have imagined about us and spoken over us instead of asking God, "Lord, what are You saying?"

God says, "For I know the thoughts that I think toward you..." (Jer. 29:11). He is saying, "I know what I'm thinking about you, and My imagination has you somewhere well away from the small, limited boundaries of men; and *what I have imagined will come to pass*."

Endnotes

1. *Strong's*, #5517 (Greek).

2. *Strong's*, #5522 (Greek).

3. *Strong's*, #5481 (Greek).

Chapter 4

Let the Wind Blow!

Jerusalem was a smoking ruin, and its great temple had just been reduced to a pile of rubble far from Ezekiel's location as an exile in Babylon. He hadn't seen his homeland in ten years. Surrounded by hopelessness and despair, the prophet Ezekiel suddenly entered the presence of God:

> *The hand of the Lord was upon me, and carried me out in the spirit of the Lord, and set me down in the midst of the valley which was full of bones, and caused me to pass by them round about: and, behold, there were very many in the open valley; and, lo, they were very dry. And He said unto me, Son of man, can these bones live? And I answered, O Lord God, Thou knowest* (Ezekiel 37:1-3).

Moments after Ezekiel saw this valley filled with scattered and parched bones, God asked him a loaded question: "Son of man, *can these bones live?*" The prophet's heart was already heavy over the pain of his nation, and the destruction of the temple. He gave the only answer that seemed to fit: "O Lord God, Thou knowest."

One thing I like about Ezekiel is that he did not infuse his own ideas or conjectures into God's vision. He simply said the truth, "God, You know. I don't even want to think about what these bones are capable of doing. I just don't know—they look like dry, disconnected bones to me; but God, You know."

Nearly every person on this planet has a lot of people trying to tell them who they are (or should be). If you're trying to live out the image conjured up by other people, then you probably feel pretty dry and disconnected, too.

"My parents want me to be this, and my girlfriend wants me to be that, Lord. My brothers want me to do this, and my boss wants me to be this, *but God, You know.*" If you don't speak to the bones of your life, they will lay there. I don't want to even think about what could happen, what should happen, or what won't happen—I just want God to have His way. When Ezekiel said, "Lord, You know," God said, "All right, prophesy! Prophesy to what you cannot see."

Again He said unto me, Prophesy upon these bones, and say unto them, O ye dry bones, hear the word of the Lord. Thus saith the Lord God unto these bones; Behold, I will cause breath to enter into you, and ye shall live: and I will lay sinews upon you, and will bring up flesh upon you, and cover you with skin, and put breath in you, and ye shall live; and ye shall know that I am the Lord (Ezekiel 37:4-6).

After Ezekiel prophesied to the bones, he probably heard his voice echoing across the valley in the deathly still air that hot afternoon. Maybe he was afraid he had wasted his breath prophesying into thin air over a valley of bones. Nothing seemed to happen at first, and all Ezekiel had to depend on was the Word of the Lord.

So I prophesied as I was commanded: and as I prophesied, there was a noise, and behold a shaking, and the bones came together, bone to his bone. And when I beheld, lo, the sinews and the flesh came up upon them, and the skin covered them above: but there was no breath in them (Ezekiel 37:7-8).

It takes faith to obey God. You have to trust God to obey God, especially when He tells you to speak to things that are intangible as well as invisible. Don't be surprised if the Lord sends you to resurrect something that has died, such as a dream or vision—while the world stands idly by, thinking you are wasting your time.

I am amazed at Christians who can believe for partial miracles. What you must understand is that the adversary is always at work, and even though you had enough faith to see the first half of what God had promised you, the devil desires to make you doubt that God will complete the work. Like Ezekiel, your problem may be that you stopped after you prophesied to the bones.

Your prophecy to the dry and scattered bones just created *bones that were connected and in order*—yet they still had no life or purpose. When something finally happens, it may seem to fall short of God's best. That is because God isn't finished yet. You may be in the right position, and you may be connected to the "right" people, but you are still in the same dry place where there's no life. Don't let the crowds of critics and doubters stop you—*prophesy to the wind!* You need to call out to God, "Let the Holy Ghost blow upon these dry bones!"

> *Then said He unto me, Prophesy unto the wind, prophesy, son of man, and say to the wind, thus saith the Lord God; Come from the four winds, O breath, and breathe upon these slain, that they may live. So I prophesied as He commanded me, and the breath came into them, and they lived, and stood up upon their feet, an exceeding great army* (Ezekiel 37:9-10).

Nothing lives without the breath of God! This is what happened in Jerusalem on the Day of Pentecost!

> *And when the day of Pentecost was fully come, they were all with one accord in one place. And suddenly there came a sound from heaven as of **a rushing mighty wind**... And they were all **filled with the Holy Ghost**...* (Acts 2:1-2,4).

You need to tell God, "Breathe on me." Without the breath of the Spirit, we cannot accomplish anything. According to Jesus, every person must be born again (Jn. 3:3).

This is God's way of resurrecting our dry bones from the valley of despair and placing us in His mighty army.

Image is everything! Every time we encounter the living God, we are changed and conformed more and more into His image. Isaiah the prophet described his life-changing encounter with God nearly a hundred years before Ezekiel:

> *In the year that king Uzziah died I saw also the Lord sitting upon a throne, high and lifted up, and His train filled the temple. ... Then said I, Woe is me! for I am undone; because I am a man of unclean lips, and I dwell in the midst of a people of unclean lips: for mine eyes have seen the King, the Lord of hosts* (Isaiah 6:1,5).

This man is saying, "In the year that king Uzziah died, *my perception of God changed!*" Isaiah was "brought up in the temple." He was the son of a prophet and the nephew of the king. "I had everything going for me, but *then I saw the Lord!* He was high and lifted up, and His glory filled the temple! After I saw Him, I looked at the earth and saw God everywhere! I saw Him in everything."

If we change the image of God, we change the image of ourselves. If we change the image of ourselves, then we change the image of our God. If I can convince you that you came from an ape, for instance, then that means the image you have of yourself (and your God) is very, very low. If, like Isaiah, you can see God as He is, then your whole image of yourself must change radically. You have to say, "If I came from Him, if I have His breath in me, then my potential is limitless!"

The first thing Isaiah did after he saw the Lord high and lifted up was to look at himself! His whole perception of himself changed once he measured himself against the glory of God. We're too busy looking at Sister Margaret to see what she is wearing, and punching the person next to us to say, "Look at Brother Jones over there—the Lord sure is convicting him! It's about time he paid his dues."

When God enters the room, when His glory floods a place, we should do exactly what Isaiah did! We should look at ourselves with new eyes and moan, "Oh, woe is me! I am unclean and unworthy!" When we look at the King of kings and then back at ourselves, we have to say, "Something is wrong here! I thought I was politically correct and religiously righteous, but once I saw Him, it changed my perception."

There are a whole lot of folks in the Church who are good Baptists, good Methodists, good Presbyterians, and good Pentecostals—the problem is that *they haven't seen the King!* They are still measuring themselves against the person sitting next to them. (It's easy to find somebody in a crowd who makes you look good.) As Isaiah discovered, everything changes when you get a glimpse of who God is!

Then said I, Woe is me! for I am undone; because I am a man of unclean lips, and I dwell in the midst of a people of unclean lips: for mine eyes have seen the King, the Lord of hosts. Then flew one of the seraphims unto me, having a live coal in his hand, which he had taken with the tongs from off the altar: and he laid it upon my mouth, and said, Lo, this hath touched thy lips; and thine iniquity is taken away, and thy sin purged. Also I heard the voice of the Lord, saying, Whom shall I send, and who will go for Us? Then said I, Here am I; send me (Isaiah 6:5-8).

Isaiah cried out, "I'm a man of unclean lips and I dwell in the midst of people with unclean lips! I can't even look at the King. I've seen something that I'm not supposed to see!" God sent an angel with a live coal from the altar of God to cleanse Isaiah's tongue and make it worthy to utter holy words. The angel said, "Your sins have been forgiven and your iniquity is purged." When Isaiah heard the Lord ask, "Whom shall I send, and who will go for Us?" this man, who only moments before perceived himself as an unclean man, said, "Here am I; send me."

What happened? When Isaiah saw the Lord as He is, he changed the image he had of himself! Now, instead of hiding from God, he ran to the front of the line to answer God's call. Any man or woman who is touched by the Master will not be the same person he or she used to be!

God uses the force of His life-giving breath to create, to bring life, to resurrect, and to empower mankind. In both the Hebrew and Greek languages, certain words used for "breath" in key passages are synonymous with spirit and wind. In the Book of Genesis, God breathed into Adam's nostrils "the *breath* of life" (Gen. 2:7). Ezekiel prophesied, "Thus saith the Lord God; Come from the four *winds*, O *breath*, and breathe upon these slain, that they may live" (Ezek. 37:9). In the Book of Acts, the arrival of the Holy Spirit in the upper room was marked by "a sound from heaven as of a rushing mighty *wind*, and it filled all the house…" (Acts 2:2). The moment the people were filled with the Holy Ghost (*pneuma* means spirit, wind, breath of life[1]), they also began to speak…. When God wants to revive something in our lives, He sends His Spirit, His wind, and His breath. It is the Spirit of God that counters the continual efforts of the devil to change our image from the holy to the unholy.

Mary was an average 13- to 15-year-old Jewish girl when God sent the angel, Gabriel, to her at her home in lowly Nazareth. The first thing the angel of God did when he saw her was to *change the image* she had of herself. Notice the salutation: "…Hail, thou that art highly favoured, the Lord is with thee: blessed art thou among women" (Lk. 1:28). It didn't matter that she was betrothed. God didn't care about her social status. It didn't matter that she was a teenage girl in a culture that did not recognize the value of women. God declared, "You are blessed above women." Mary was troubled and fearful when she saw Gabriel, but he spoke the words of God, saying, "Fear not, Mary: for thou hast found favour with God" (Lk. 1:30).

When Mary asked Gabriel how she could give birth to a son while still a virgin, the angel said, "The Holy Ghost [*Pneuma Hagios*] shall come upon thee, and the power of the Highest shall overshadow thee: therefore also that holy thing which shall be born of thee shall be called the Son of God" (Lk. 1:35). Once again the Spirit, the Breath, and the Wind of God invaded the natural realm of mankind to effect God's will.

God raised Mary's image of herself, and He accomplished His purpose in her through His Spirit. Her response is a model for everyone who is confronted with what seems to be an impossible destiny or task by the Spirit of God. She said, "Behold the handmaid of the Lord; be it unto me according to thy word" (Lk. 1:38b).

Mary was saying, "God, I'm going to believe what You say about me. If You say I am highly favored, then I'm going to walk in that. If You tell me I am blessed, then I'm going to walk in that. If You tell me that You have chosen me, then I'm going to walk in that." She knew from the angel's words that she would have to go through some hard times. She would have to give up her child for her nation. She could probably see herself walking through the streets of little Nazareth, trying to explain something that was impossible to explain. "Mary, you claim that you are still a virgin, yet you are obviously pregnant. Something is obviously wrong here." She could visualize her awkward attempts to answer questions, "You wouldn't understand. You see, it was an angel; and I said, 'Let it be according to thy word,' and this is what happened!" She could also visualize the response of her friends and family, "Okay, Mary, if you say so...."

Every one of us will face tests and trials when we respond to God's Spirit with her words, "Be it unto me according to Thy word." We will all face difficult moments of truth standing over a pile of dead bones, dreams, or ministry plans we have just prophesied over—praying that some sign of life will spring up quickly. We will face the cynical questions and barbed comments of disapproving friends, families, and enemies who just don't understand the work of God in our lives.

That is why we must find ourselves in the company of those who understand the voice of God. Mary left home after this epiphany and ran to the house of her cousin Elizabeth who, months earlier, also had a visitation from Gabriel. How did Elizabeth greet Mary? The same way the angel greeted Mary! "Blessed art thou among women...." Don't be discouraged if others don't recognize you for who God says you are. It takes the Spirit of God to reveal the *new you!*

You and I have no business down-rating what God has manifested in us and others! Remember, when you change the image of yourself, you change the image of your God. The Lord has placed great potential in you and I, and He wants to make us great! He places us in the company of other great people, yet we sit complaining about what we are unable to do, or what people won't allow us to do. Read carefully now what Jesus says to His disciples:

> *And the disciples came, and said unto Him, Why speakest Thou unto them in parables? He answered and said unto them, Because it is given unto you to know the mysteries of the kingdom of heaven, but to them it is not given. For whosoever hath, to him shall be given, and he shall have more abundance: but whosoever hath not, from him shall be taken away even that he hath. Therefore speak I to them in parables: because they seeing see not; and hearing they hear not, neither do they understand* (Matthew 13:10-13).

Jesus said the mysteries of the Kingdom that others misunderstand should be clearly understood by you. That is why I don't ascribe to the concept that we please God by being poor and poverty-stricken.

God said He would add to the little bit of faith, talent, wealth, or vision that I have—if I invest it in Him and in His will. Jesus said, "For whosoever hath, to him shall be given, and he shall have more abundance: but whosoever hath not, from him shall be taken away even that he hath" (Mt. 13:12).

This promise should make you want to tell your critics and naysayers: "If you're upset right now because you think I have something I don't deserve, just watch. If you didn't like me before, then you won't want to have anything to do with me in a little while! No, it's not because of me—it is because of the image that I have of Him who created me! When I lift Him up, He lifts me up! I have recognized that the earth is the Lord's and the fullness thereof, and the worlds and they that dwell therein. When I see how great God is, and when I look at what God has given me to work with, I just want to be like Him in every way!"

Compare the confession you just read with this statement: "I don't have anything, and I'm not going to be anything or get anything either. I just don't know why God treats me so bad." Which confession is true to the Bible? Which confession is closest to the imagination of God?

People tend to get mad at the few individuals who excel and succeed, who dare to stand out through achievement and vision. Yet these people have simply recognized what

God has placed within them, and they are working with it to produce fruit. Now when God sees you hiding what He gave you in a napkin and burying it under a mound of complaints, crying, and negative words about what you *don't have*, He says, "Give Me what you *do have*—I'm going to give it to somebody who sees greatness in himself! I'll give it to someone who sees power in himself and recognizes Me as the Creator of the ends of the earth."

You need to recognize that God has put a treasure in you as an "earthen vessel" (see 2 Cor. 4:7). You have to reach down within yourself to find the treasure of God that is buried there. Wherever there is treasure, there is *work* involved. You have to get your shovel and do some digging if you want to come up with God's gold! It's in there. It just takes the working of faith to bring it up into the light. That treasure may be buried beneath abuse or past hurts. It may be buried beneath a smothering alcohol addiction, or beneath a stubborn drug habit. Many of us find it buried beneath our low self-esteem, or beneath a life of sin. No matter how deeply God's treasure is buried, the Word of God gives you everything you need to find it and bring it into the light. There is a precious and holy treasure hidden within you that God has ordained for greatness, but first you must be purged to be like Him.

That is why no believer can afford to be comfortable with sin—it buries the treasure. Sin buries who you really are and alters your state. It changes you from what God intended you to be into a tainted or defiled image.

God started the process when He said, "Let Us make man in Our image." He said, "Let Us make an exact copy of who We are, and let Us stamp Our image inside him." Whenever we change the image of ourselves from the image God stamped in us, we must erase God's image and impression and substitute it with something else that doesn't conflict with our sin.

The reason we have so many idols or images in America today is because we have become comfortable with so many different things that are contrary to God's plan and priorities. We think we can make a god to fit whatever it is we are doing at the time. Paul told the men of Athens, "I perceive that in all things ye are too superstitious" (Acts 17:22b). The Athenians had a god for everything. There was a god for the sun, for the moon, and for the stars. There was a god of thunder, a god of lightning, and a god of rain. There were also gods for corn, wheat, and the harvest; and a god of fertility. Our modern society has just as many gods as the ancient Greeks! We created them in our own fallen image to make our sin comfortable and to shield us from the revealing light of God's true image.

I'm telling you that you are *more than you thought you were*. You may have been born in the image of a fallen father, of the seed of sinful man, but when God saves you, *He changes the image you have of you*! Paul put it this way: "Therefore if any man be in Christ, he is a new creature [with a new image of himself—he can't look at himself like he used to look at himself because]: old things are passed away; behold, all things [and especially his image] are become new" (2 Cor. 5:17). I used to think of myself as a pile of dirt, as a dry bone lost in a valley of desolation, but because I've been touched by the breath of God, I have a new image, a new life, and a new future!

Why is your image changed? You have seen the King! Like the prophet Isaiah, you have seen the Lord high and lifted up. You have discovered how much power He has. When He speaks, the doorposts of His temple shake. Your God is holy, all-knowing, and all-powerful. After He touched you, you began to realize who you are. You have been made in His image and likeness and stamped with His greatness and power. You have been endued with power from on High by the very breath and wind of God's Spirit. Now if God needs somebody, you can't help yourself! You step to the front of the line and say, "Lord, here I am! Use me! Let me be the instrument of Your peace. Let me bring You glory through my weakness and my dependence on You. I can go on Your behalf and in Your name. I can get the job done as long as I have Your image."

Like Ezekiel standing in a valley filled with bleached and disjointed bones, you step forward, fill your lungs with air, and prophesy to the winds of God! "Yes, in Jesus' name, I can go and cast out devils. I can heal the sick! I can preach repentance to sinners, and deliverance to the captives! I am anointed to convert souls to the light. Why? Because I am like You, Lord!"

Endnote

1. *Strong's*, #4151, #4157 (Greek).

Chapter 5

That's Not What We Heard!

The image of God is offensive to anything and everything that sets itself up as its own standard of perfection. The term, "pecking order," comes from the behavior of chicks and chickens, where the strong peck at the weak. If one chick is too different from the rest, the majority will literally peck it to death. I've observed that human beings act like chickens at times.

If someone walks into a room who looks nicer, talks better, sings better, or is more popular than you, do you feel the "urge" to stare at him and pick at him until you find a flaw to "bring him down to your level"? Now be honest. You know you've felt that kind of urge before.

Jesus knows about this human trait because when He came to earth, He was totally different from the rest of us. He had a different Father whom no one had ever seen but Him. His birth had been announced and the details of His coming had been memorized by religious scholars for hundreds of years before He came, yet He was recognized and welcomed by only a handful of people, some of whom were even foreigners! There were no other boys close to His age, for every other male child born at the same time as He had died at the hands of a jealous king years before. He seemed to have an inside knowledge of the ancient scrolls that made Him stand out from the rest of the boys studying the Torah—and it didn't make Him popular either.

The biggest problems centered around His past. Everyone in that small village knew that His mother became pregnant long before she and Joseph began to live together as husband and wife. Of course, Joseph claimed Jesus as his own, and treated Him that way, but the village gossips just couldn't let such a juicy tidbit go to waste. Whenever Jesus' childhood companions felt like it, they would bring up His past. This really began to happen after He began His adult ministry and returned to His hometown synagogue. His old playmates felt obligated to bring this "upstart" back down to earth:

> "Jesus, You claim to be the son of David and the Son of God—**but that's not what we heard**! You can work all the miracles You want to work, but look, we remember when Your *step*-daddy (we still haven't found out who Your *real* daddy is) and Your mother had to get out of town.

> "You can fool all those folks in other cities, but we were here. You can't fool Your hometown folks in Nazareth, because *we know how You got here*. So don't come here and try to say You are the Son of God! That's just not what we heard. No, we

have to try to change that image back to the earthbound image we have of You."

Even the one perfect man who walked the earth was unable to please everybody. Jesus Christ was without sin. He was perfect, He was love incarnate, and He possessed all wisdom, yet Jesus had to deal with His past, too! We should expect to run into opposition and rejection along the way as well. Even Jesus had to deal with it. This should be an encouragement to us.

I discovered the importance of image the hard way, through a serious, long-term trial that caused me to examine everything about my ministry, my identity, and my relationship with God. It is more than just a "good message" to me—it is a truth I received directly from God in answer to my prayers birthed in painful struggle.

I couldn't understand what I was going through, or why it was happening to me. It just didn't seem to make sense. I was only trying to do what God had been telling me to do, and I was doing everything I knew to do, but people repeatedly told me, "You've got a pride problem. *You just think you are something* (when you're not)."

About ten years ago, I told my brothers that the day would come in about three years when I would no longer tour with our singing group, "The Winans." They thought I was kidding at first. We have enjoyed tremendous success over the past 16 years of ministry, receiving six Grammy Awards, numerous Dove Awards, and a "gold record" along the way. Yet I knew God was calling me to something more.

The greatest trials in my life came when I answered God's call to pastor. I've always loved to hear the preaching of the gospel, but I really didn't want to preach or pastor. My grandfather, and his father before him, were pastors. I knew firsthand just how hard and difficult the pastorate could be. I finally surrendered to God's call and launched "Perfecting Church" in my hometown of Detroit, Michigan, with eight people in my basement. At the time of this writing, the Perfecting Church body had just moved into a facility that is four city blocks long to accommodate our growth and vision for ministry to inner-city Detroit! God has blessed us, but first I had to face *a devastating attack on my image!*

I was deeply hurt and troubled each time I heard someone tell me, "Marvin, you think you are *somebody*." Anybody who really knows me will tell you that is the furthest thing from the truth. I am unimpressed with stars and celebrities. I dearly love them as people, but I tend to be unimpressed with titles, awards, or sales figures. Over the years, our family has met and befriended countless musicians, recording artists, actors, and movie stars. We have shared the stage and the TV lights with most of them at one time or another.

I was asked to conduct the marriage ceremony for Whitney Houston and Bobby Brown, and when they completed their vows, all the movie stars, TV actors, and recording artists were coming into the house for the wedding reception. The only thing I wanted to know was, "Where is my car? I have to catch my flight for Detroit—I'm going home." When I got home and watched the evening news, I saw video footage of all the news helicopters flying over the house and photographers scrambling to take pictures of Whitney and Bobby. The whole time that was going on, I was on a plane going home.

I love Whitney and Bobby, but once the wedding was over, I wanted to be home with the people of God more than to stay someplace just to "rub shoulders" with the rich and famous guests for the sake of "being somebody."

Again and again, I heard the cutting criticism leveled at me, "Winans, you think you are somebody, don't you?" This trial continually wore on my spirit and eroded my confidence until the Holy Ghost spoke to my heart, saying, "Marvin, listen to what they are saying: 'You think you are somebody.' " Then the Lord spoke directly to my accuser using my lips, *"You will not make me change the image I have of myself!"*

The Lord told me, "Marvin, in and of yourself, you are no better than anyone else. The man standing on the freeway ramp holding a sign, or the homeless person pushing the shopping cart down the sidewalk—that could be you. What is the difference? The difference is that *you decided to believe what I have said about you!"*

> *...I ordained thee a prophet unto the nations. Then said I, Ah, Lord God! behold, I cannot speak: for I am a child. But the Lord said unto me, Say not, I am a child: for thou shalt go to all that I shall send thee, and whatsoever I command thee thou shalt speak. Be not afraid of their faces: for I am with thee to deliver thee, saith the Lord. Then the Lord put forth His hand, and touched my*

mouth. And the Lord said unto me, Behold, I have put My words in thy mouth. See, I have this day set thee over the nations... (Jeremiah 1:5-10).

Regardless of what situation or difficulty I find myself in, I have learned, like the prophet Jeremiah, to say what God says. Jeremiah told the Lord, "I'm a child. I don't have the ability." God told him not to say he was a child, for He had put His word in his mouth! He told Jeremiah that he had been separated unto God from his mother's womb to be a prophet to the nations. He basically told Jeremiah, "Now you say what I say. See yourself as I see you."

After obeying God, Jeremiah found himself bruised and bound in stocks at a city gate. In exasperation, Jeremiah said, "You didn't tell me about this! I quit."

*O Lord, Thou hast deceived me, and I was deceived: Thou art stronger than I, and hast prevailed: I am in derision daily, every one mocketh me. ...because the word of the Lord was made a reproach unto me.... Then [Jeremiah] said, I will not make mention of Him, nor speak any more in His name. **But His word was in mine heart as a burning fire shut up in my bones,** and I was weary with forbearing, and I could not stay* (Jeremiah 20:7-9).

Jeremiah said, "God, I quit. That's it. I'm going home. I'm sick of the abuse. I'm tired." When he got home, the Bible says the word of God was in his heart like a burning fire. Just the effort of trying to resist God's call wore him out, so Jeremiah got back up and said, "I have to do what I was born to do—I have no choice, because God's word is like a burning fire shut up in my bones." This is still another proof of the Scripture passage that says, "For as [a man] thinketh in his heart, so is he" (Prov. 23:7a).

The enemy doesn't want you to think you are smart enough, strong enough, or wise enough to succeed in anything but failure. He especially doesn't want you to see yourself as God made you—in His image. He wants you to see yourself as a "pilgrim of sorrow," always doomed to climb up the rough side of the mountain, accepting "whatever comes."

He doesn't want you to see yourself as a mighty man or woman of God. He wants you to walk around in perpetual depression, expecting the worst and accepting everything he dishes out to you (while saying that "God did it"). He wants your anthem to be, "Lord, any way You bless me I am satisfied, I guess." (The problem is that there is a big difference between God's blessings and the devil's messings!) Above all, the enemy of your soul wants to erase the destiny God spoke over mankind in the garden, and again after the resurrection of Jesus Christ. The devil doesn't want you to see yourself as a *conquering king.*

God did *not* call us to be "pilgrims of sorrow"; He has appointed us to be a nation of kings and priests! Yet, if you dare to speak the truth as God sees it, don't be shocked when the devil stirs up people (yes, even *good people*) to shout back at you, "That's not what we heard!"

God says you *are* going to be somebody, but that can only happen if you *see yourself* in that place. You have to walk in God's image, not your own. You have to talk God's talk, not your own. Speak the things He says, not the things others say. I have to warn you that this kind of commitment will make you "stick out" from the rest of the pack, so hold on.

God made me a dreamer. I love to think big like my big God. I've learned that my dreams carry a big price tag at times. People look at me, and they hear me talking about reaching thousands for Christ, or establishing a school, or reaching out to substance abusers and street people, and they say, "See, he is just cocky!" No, I'm not cocky, but neither do I have the time or permission from God to ask my critics, "Can I do this? Do I have your permission and support to obey God?"

I openly confess to my congregation, *I have absolutely no business doing what I do.* I don't have a college degree, and I didn't go to any seminary (no, I'm not against college degrees or education). The fact is that no one can accomplish the will of God apart from His grace and supernatural provision. College degrees won't do it. Official credentials won't do it. Friendships and professional associations won't do it. Even natural gifts for administration, preaching, and the supernatural gifts won't do it. You can't build a ministry on your gifts; it must be built on the Rock Himself, Jesus Christ.

I'm convinced that God loves to put us in situations and callings that push us beyond our natural ability, training, or resources because it brings Him all the glory. Just knowing this fact doesn't help make it any easier, though. It can be frightening at times.

One time when I was recording an album, we needed a fully orchestrated string background behind our vocals. A good friend (who is one of the few black conductors in Chicago) scored it for me. When I went to Chicago to record it, the concert master of the Chicago Symphony Orchestra was playing along with several other professional concert musicians he had contracted for the session.

You know how snobbish some musicians can be, especially when they are "learned musicians" in classical music. We had prerecorded the vocals to "Worthy Is the Lamb" at our church in Detroit, and these musicians were trying to lay in the string sections. My friend Paul asked me to step into the studio and conduct the group for a trial run just to give the concert master the timing and "feel" for the introductory measures and whatnot.

A lady in the group asked out loud, "Is he a conductor?" Paul replied, "No," and then looked at me and added, "But you do it anyway, Marvin." I just shook my head and went back into the studio control room and sat down. I didn't want to cause any problems, and it didn't hurt my feelings anyway. I knew I wasn't a conductor when I came there. To make a long story short, they tried and tried to play that orchestration, but they just couldn't get it right. (They kept missing the beat and messing up the whole thing.)

Finally the concert master asked Paul to have me come out. "Marvin," I heard over the microphone, "would you come out here?" No, I didn't have a degree in music or in music theory, and I had never conducted an orchestra of any kind or size. But I was saved and I was humble by the grace of God. The one thing I knew was that God had put His music inside me.

I went out there and took the baton while everyone watched me. I didn't know anything about conducting a symphony orchestra, but I knew I had been given this music to touch broken lives and to lift up God's name. I took a deep breath, lifted the baton with a flare, and proceeded to "conduct" that studio orchestra into the very presence of God. You have to see yourself as God sees you because...*image is everything!*

The apostle Paul told the church at Corinth, "And so it is written, The first man Adam was made a living soul; the last Adam was made a quickening spirit" (1 Cor. 15:45). Adam was made in the image of God, but the second Adam *was* the "express image" of God Himself.

> [God] *hath in these last days spoken unto us by His Son, whom He hath appointed heir of all things, by whom also He made the worlds; who being the brightness of His glory, and the **express image of His person**, and upholding all things by the word of His power, when He had by Himself purged our sins, sat down on the right hand of the Majesty on high* (Hebrews 1:2-3).

Although the first Adam was "made man like unto God," the second Adam was "God made like unto man." Do you see the difference? The first Adam had an identity crisis, but the second Adam boldly told His accusers, "Though I bear record of Myself, yet My record is true: *for I know whence I came*, and whither I go; but ye cannot tell whence I come, and whither I go" (Jn. 8:14).

The enemy did everything he could to invalidate the Lord's claim to deity and to stop His mission of redemption. He stirred up devout Jews to shout in religious anger, "How dare You talk like You've been with God!" The Lord called things as they were, and He exposed the source of his attackers' words:

> *Jesus said unto them, If God were your Father, ye would love Me: for I proceeded forth and came from God; neither came I of Myself, but He sent Me. Why do ye not understand My speech? even because ye cannot hear My word. Ye are of your father the devil, and the lusts of your father ye will do...* (John 8:42-44).

People don't like hearing the truth. The "Express Image" of God made them uncomfortable with the sins they had worked so hard to hide behind their religion! When they gave Him a number of excuses and religious reasons to justify their sins, Jesus said, "If ye were Abraham's children, ye would do the works of Abraham. But now ye seek to kill Me, a man that hath told you the truth.... Your father Abraham rejoiced to see My day: and he saw it, and was glad" (Jn. 8:39-40,56). They said in rising anger, *"That's not what we heard!"* (the Marvin Winans' version).

Once again, satan incited the people to attack the image of God in Jesus by saying, in effect, "What are You talking about? You are not even 50 years old and Abraham has been dead for centuries!" Jesus refused to let His image be changed, and the people lost control of themselves in their efforts to hold on to the tarnished and broken image satan had convinced them was God's ultimate image of perfection.

This same problem afflicts the Church today. When God gives us a vision of His image, and a vision of His purpose for us in our generation, we share our vision with others and run into opposition. Then we get discouraged and disenchanted because we look at our negative circumstances. Can you imagine what would have happened had Jesus looked at Himself and His problems instead of fixing His eyes on His Father? What if Jesus had not looked at what God had placed in Him?

For the first time in all eternity, God (in Christ) knew what it felt like for a body to grow weak. He knew what it was like to be gripped by fatigue, to have to fight off disease and infection like other humans. The body of the Savior had to go through pain just like other humans. Jesus wasn't numb during the beatings and the crucifixion—He experienced excruciating pain! He knew what it was to experience desertion, and He felt the bruising and crushing pain of the brutal beating He endured. His body experienced the piercing pain of being cruelly spiked with a nail and hammer. He felt the humiliation and shame of being spat upon. Can you imagine what life would be like today if our salvation had not been sealed because Jesus *looked at the safety and needs of His body* instead of the will of His Father?

Ever since God established order in His created world, the devil has tried to bring disorder. We are living in a very evil time. Anytime you lift up God's image in a distorted world, you will meet opposition. Paul put it this way: "Yea, and all that will live godly in Christ Jesus shall suffer persecution" (2 Tim. 3:12).

Jesus ran into trouble because He went straight for the heart. He never settled for mere appearances or words of righteousness. He said, "...whosoever looketh on a woman to lust after her hath committed adultery with her already in his heart" (Mt. 5:28). That's pretty strict, and it eliminates every loophole. God judges the heart and thoughts while man only judges outward actions.

Man is easily fooled because he is controlled by his senses. God cannot be fooled or deceived; He understands what is beneath the surface. The judgment of the Lord is true—but it is rarely popular! Anyone who chooses to live according to God's image is sure to arouse some opposition along the way.

To have the image of God means that we are shadowed by God. It means that we resemble Him. It means that we are made in His likeness, like an engraving or representative, an illusion of Him. When the world sees us, they should see God. We need to be prepared for rejection, for it will come. God is calling us to persevere and press through for His glory. That is how we reach the lost: by living godly and with love, even in the face of ungodly, unloving responses.

People are looking for the real thing in the world, and the "real thing" stands out best in times of trouble and hardship. The God in you shows up best when the "human" in you has given out! Then people can know that you really do know God, because He is the One who is carrying you through and making you *different* from everyone else around you!

I want to say again that when the world sees us, they should see God. Jesus said, "As long as I am in the world, I am the light of the world" (Jn. 9:5). He also said, "Ye are the light of the world. ... Let your light so shine before men, that they may see your good works, and glorify your Father which is in heaven" (Mt. 5:14a,16). The world should see God every time they see us.

As we noted before, embracing God's vision and image carries a risk with it. Chapter 37 of the Book of Genesis records the story of Joseph. The youngest son of Jacob/Israel, he was sold into slavery by his own brothers after he dared to share a dream God had given him.

> *And he dreamed yet another dream, and told it his brethren, and said, Behold, I have dreamed a dream more; and, behold, the sun and the moon and the eleven stars made obeisance to me. And he told it to his father, and to his brethren: and his father rebuked him, and said unto him, What is this dream that thou hast dreamed? Shall I and thy mother and thy brethren indeed come to bow down ourselves to thee to the earth?* (Genesis 37:9-10).

Joseph didn't get very many hearty "amens" and "hallelujahs" that day. Perhaps he was too hasty in sharing his heavenly vision, but God was in it nonetheless. His father, mother, and brothers were very fortunate that Joseph stuck with that vision through the pit, the prison, and the adversity of Egypt. He was their ticket to God's blessing in the troubled times of famine in the years ahead.

The devil has tried to disrupt the order of God since his first unsuccessful act of rebellion in Heaven. His dark kingdom is organized to disorganize. Yet God is not the author of confusion, and He always gives His people a vision and an image of what He wants us to be and do. God wants to give each of us a clear picture of Himself. He wants us to understand the image.

We live in a very confused society that doesn't want God's order because it reveals the dark deeds of men in their depravity. Proverbs 21:30 says, "There is no wisdom nor understanding nor counsel against the Lord."

I don't care how many college degrees a man has, or how many graduate classes he is taking. It doesn't matter how many years a person has studied human psychology and human behavior patterns. The Bible warns about men who, "professing themselves to be wise, they became fools, and *changed* the glory of the uncorruptible God *into an image* made like to corruptible man, and to birds, and four-footed beasts, and creeping things" (Rom. 1:22-23).

Now, the devil takes his time. He is a deceiver with no virtue, but he has a small measure of patience. He will spend years trying to convince you of one thing if he thinks he can steal or distort your image! As the father of lies, he knows that to effectively deceive you, he has to mingle untruth with truth. He carefully forms his lies to at least give the perception of truth. That is why satan tried to tempt Jesus in the wilderness by quoting the Scriptures!

The greatest travesty in the world is the failure of people who *know the truth* to actually *obey and follow the truth*! Paul was talking about people who knew the Scriptures when he wrote, "For the wrath of God is revealed from heaven against all ungodliness and unrighteousness of men, who hold the truth in unrighteousness" (Rom. 1:18). The greatest opposition against Jesus Christ, and later against Paul and the other disciples, did not come from the unlearned or the "unchurched"—it came from religious people who had been thoroughly exposed to the truth of God's Word! Once you begin to walk in the image of God, you will almost certainly face opposition. When you begin to say the things God says about you, don't be surprised if you hear that familiar line from those who have known you most of your life: "That's not what I heard!"

Chapter 6

Don't Let My Flesh
Fool You!

In the previous chapter, we found that anyone who dares to live godly will experience persecution. In this chapter, we will learn how Jesus handled persecution and stopped satan's efforts to steal and distort His image.

Satan wanted to strip Jesus of His identity more than anything else! He hoped to strike quickly at the human part of Jesus during the 40 days of temptation in the wilderness early in Christ's ministry. His aim was to take advantage of Jesus during this unfamiliar time of weakness. I want to examine in detail the events of this passage in Matthew chapter 4.

"Then was Jesus led up of the spirit into the wilderness..." (Mt. 4:1). The first thing we note is that the Spirit led Jesus (the Word) into the wilderness. It is easy for us to know who we are in familiar places where people constantly remind us of who we are. But the Spirit will drive you into a place where the Word is the only thing you have to stand on.

"And when He had fasted forty days and forty nights, He was afterward an hungered" (Mt. 4:2). Again, the devil seeks you out when you are hungry; hunger represents need and deprivation. He will only seek you out when you are weak and vulnerable. This statement is confirmed in First Peter 5:8: "Be sober, be vigilant; because *your* adversary the devil, *as a roaring lion*, walketh about, seeking whom he *may* devour."

The tempter only preys upon the helpless and hurting. Thinking that this was the case with Jesus, he said, "If Thou be the Son of God, command that these stones be made bread" (Mt. 4:3). Notice the first line of satan's attack was to the image—not to His body, not to His economic status—but to the image that Jesus had of Himself.

"If Thou be the Son of God…." The devil was testing the waters. Jesus had not spoken to anyone as to His true identity. He only had the witness of John the Baptist and God the Father when He spoke from Heaven declaring that Jesus was in fact His beloved Son in whom He was well pleased. What I have discovered is that it matters not what God says about you and I if we do not believe it.

Lucifer was well aware of what was spoken by John the Baptist and what was thundered from Heaven. But what he did not know was whether or not Jesus would believe and operate in what the Father had said about Him. Jesus replied,

"Man shall not live by bread alone, but by every *word* that proceedeth out of the mouth of God" (Mt. 4:4b). What Jesus was declaring to the enemy was His intention to live in the realm to which He was called. Despite the obvious contradiction He would receive from the religious community, He was declaring His God-given right to operate as the Son of God in the earth.

The devil must have thought that Jesus would be like so many of the other men he had brought to ruin through temptation. He had aimed at their natural appetites, their lust for recognition, power, and fame, and made deceptive appeals to pride. (After all, he would do anything for pride's sake—even rebel against the Most High.)

Each time the enemy came to Jesus with a temptation, Jesus answered him from the Word of God. The Lord's answer to the final temptation reveals the importance of image in any situation involving temptation:

> *And the devil said unto Him, All this power will I give Thee, and the glory of them: for that is delivered unto me; and to whomsoever I will I give it. If Thou therefore wilt worship me, all shall be Thine. And Jesus answered and said unto him, Get thee behind Me, Satan: for it is written, Thou shalt worship the Lord thy God, and Him only shalt thou serve (Luke 4:6-8).*

The Lord refused to lower Himself to satan's level. He knew exactly who the Scriptures were referring to when they said, "Thou shalt worship the Lord thy God." They were referring to God—God the Father, God the Son, and God the

Holy Spirit! Jesus was saying, "Devil, even though I am in the flesh, I am still God in flesh! Don't let My flesh fool you."

You need to learn how to tell the devil the *same thing*! You need to tell him every time he comes around with temptations or accusations, "I know what it looks like, but don't let this flesh fool you! Haven't you heard the Word? God says, 'Greater is He that is in me, than he that is in the world'!"

You may have a sickness attacking your body this moment, and the devil wants to use that sickness to *change the image that you have of yourself!* Stand up in Christ and tell him, "I am the healed, and not the sick. Don't let this sickness fool you. I'm still the servant of the Most High God, and I still have all authority over you in Jesus' name!"

Are you going through a stressful financial difficulty? I can almost guarantee that the devil is trying to use it as an opportunity to make you *change the image that you have of yourself.* Don't give up, and don't give in! Give your enemy a "spiritual reality check." Tell him, "I am the blessed, above only and never beneath! Devil, don't let this situation and circumstance fool you! I'm still the same person that *God says I am*, and you're still the liar God says you are!"

Imagine, if you can, a childhood friend, a family who lived down the street from you, someone you played with or went to school with. He is an only child. The years pass; you grow up and go away to college. After completing your scholastic requirements, you receive your degree and return home only to discover that the "quiet boy" whom you played with as a child is now declaring he is the "only begotten Son of God" (see Jn. 3:16). He has garnered a reputation for healing the sick, casting out devils, restoring sight to the blind, and a cadre of spectacular feats.

As we look into the Gospels, we notice that the men and women of Jesus' era were not upset with the good He did. The persecution came when He spoke of Himself as being "one with God."

> *I and My Father are one. Then the Jews took up stones again to stone Him. Jesus answered them, Many good works have I shewed you from My Father; for which of those works do ye stone Me? The Jews answered Him, saying, For a good work we stone Thee not; but for blasphemy; and because that Thou, being a man, makest Thyself God* (John 10:30-33).

This truth is what separates Christianity from every other religion in the world. If you do not believe in the divinity of Jesus of Nazareth, then you cannot be a Christian. The true believer cannot accept any other doctrine or faith that teaches otherwise. It is this statement ("I and the Father are one"), and the teachings that supported this truth, that caused many of the Lord's followers to walk away from Him and never walk with Him again (see Jn. 6:66).

From the first day Jesus launched His ministry in the synagogue in Galilee to His last moments on the cross, people called Him names because He dared to reveal Himself as the express image of God.

"Oh, that Jesus is just a bastard."

"No, He's worse than that! That impostor is beelzebub—the prince of flies himself!"

"Didn't He cast out devils?"

"Oh sure, but don't you realize that He cast out devils by the spirit of the devil that is in Him? Don't believe His words about His identity. He is nothing."

Toward the end of His earthly ministry, Jesus told His disciples that He was about to go away to prepare a place for them (see Jn. 14:1-4). Then He revealed three more names to help His disciples understand His true identity and purpose in the earth: "I am the way, the truth, and the life: no man cometh unto the Father, but by Me" (Jn. 14:6).

Despite His clear statement that if the disciples knew Him, they then knew the Father, Philip still told the Lord, "Shew us the Father, and it sufficeth [will satisfy] us" (Jn. 14:8). He was saying, "Jesus, we've been following You for about three years now, and we have really enjoyed it. But we would be satisfied if You would just show us the Father—then we could really believe in You. We all heard about the Mount of Transfiguration from Peter, James, and John. They said they saw Elijah and Moses talking to You. They even claimed that they heard a voice saying, 'This is My beloved Son, in whom I am well pleased.' Yes, Lord, our curiosity (and all our secret doubts about You) would finally be satisfied if You would just show us the Father." It was the wrong thing to say to a man who was so secure in His image.

Jesus turned to Philip and basically said, "How long have I been with you? Why are you asking Me a silly question like that? I can't believe you're saying, 'Show us the Father and we will believe on You and we'll be satisfied!' Don't you know that when you see Me you see the Father?" (see Jn. 14:9) He was saying, "I am the best picture that God ever took. I am the *express image* of God the Father."

> *God, who at sundry times and in divers manners spake in time past unto the fathers by the prophets, hath in these last days spoken unto us by His Son, whom He hath appointed heir of all things, by whom also He made the worlds; who being the brightness of His glory, and the **express image** of His person, and upholding all things by the word of His power, when He had by Himself purged our sins, sat down on the right hand of the Majesty on high* (Hebrews 1:1-3).

In the beginning was God, and God was the Word. Jesus said, "I can speak because I was sent and delivered by the determinate counsel of God Almighty. I was daily the delight of my Father. I was with Him in the inhabitable parts of the earth. Before He threw the north in an empty space, stretched out the heavens like a curtain, and weighed the mountains in the balance; even before He decided to make the seas, I was with one with Him" (see Is. 40; Jn. 1:1; Acts 2:23).

You cannot separate God from His Word. When the Word stepped out of God, He stepped into a body and that body was given a name. There is no other name under heaven by which men can be saved except the name of Jesus (see Acts 4:12). So when Jesus speaks, everyone must listen. Jesus was saying, "I know the will of God because I came from God. I have the right to speak on God's behalf" (Jn. 7:16-17,29). When He entered a human body, He was made a little bit lower than the angels, but it did not change who He was.

From the first temptation delivered in the wilderness to the Lord's final words on the cross, the words and actions of Jesus were declaring, "Satan, no matter what you say or do, you are not going to change My mind about who I am. You are not going to change My image, and you will not stop Me from doing My Father's will and glorifying His name! I am not worried about what is going on right now. I am going to maintain My focus and fulfill My mission."

The Bible says Jesus, the author and finisher of our faith, "for the joy that was set before Him endured the cross, despising the shame" (Heb. 12:2). Jesus withstood every on-slaught of the enemy, and having done all to stand, He stood His ground because He knew who He was.

You are not going to change My image. You are not going to change whom I know God has said that I am. If I go hungry, I am still the Bread of life. If I am thirsty, I am still the eternal Spring of living water. If I'm bruised, I'm still the Healer. If I am betrayed, I am still the Faithful and True Witness. Acquainted with sorrow, I am still the Comforter. Though I bear sin and am falsely accused, I am still the Righteousness of God, the Lamb who takes away the sins of the world. I know who I am. I am the express image of God!

The Greek word for "image" is *charakter*. This is the root of our English word, *character*. The Greek word has two meanings. It refers to the *instrument* used for engraving or carving, and also refers to *the mark stamped,* a mark or figure burned in, *the exact expression* of any person or thing, and *precise reproduction in every respect.*[1] In other words, Jesus was "the stamped out image, the exact copy" of God! I know the Jehovah Witnesses don't want you to believe that. I know the Nation of Islam doesn't want you to believe it, but Jesus Christ wasn't "just another prophet"! He wasn't just another revolutionary. Jesus was the *exact copy of God.*

The doubt and unbelief of the disciples was especially troubling to Jesus. He invested three-and-a-half years of intense training with them because He knew that *where there is no successor, there is no success.* Jesus would not leave until He had transmitted what He had into someone else. He spent His time and ministry imparting His anointing and His Father's words to 12 renegades from every walk of life. For the most part, they had no formal religious training. Jesus had them walk with Him, eat with Him, and share His life with them. He told them:

> *Believe Me that I am in the Father, and the Father in Me: or else believe Me for the very works' sake. Verily, verily, I say unto you, He that believeth on Me, the works that I do shall He do also; and **greater works than these shall he do; because I go unto My Father.** And whatsoever ye shall ask in My name, that will I do, that the Father may be glorified in the Son. If ye shall ask any thing in My name, I will do it* (John 14:11-14).

Jesus told His disciples, "I'm going to give you the same thing that I have. No, this isn't a diluted, hand-me-down, second-generation anointing—I want to impart into you the same thing that is in Me."

After Jesus ascended to the Father, His disciples stayed in the upper room until they were "endued with power from on high" as Jesus promised (Lk. 24:49). They stayed up there until they knew they had the *same thing* Jesus had! Scripture says, "Ye shall know them by their fruits" (Mt. 7:16a). When the 120 believers finally left the upper room in Jerusalem, their loud proclamation of God's wonders in other tongues drew a large crowd of people. Peter stood up and boldly addressed the crowd without fear—the same man who lied and cursed when challenged by a housemaid only days before. What had happened? This man *received what God has!* He wasn't afraid any longer.

Peter told the crowd, "For these are not drunken, as ye suppose.... But *this is that* which was spoken by the prophet Joel" (Acts 2:15-16), speaking of the baptism of the Holy Spirit. Jesus promised His disciples He would send a Comforter, a Teacher, and a Guide when He returned to His Father in Heaven (see Jn. 16:7-15).

He told them, "As long as I'm in the world, I'm the light of the world; but when I leave, guess what? I'm giving you a *different image.* Some of you have been fishermen, but you were only fishing for fish. I'm going to change the image that you have of yourself. You are not going to be fishing for fish anymore; you are going to become fishers of men! I have to *change your image.*"

Now, the wonderful thing about Jesus is that He never simply talked—He walked. He was our *example.* Jesus, the second Adam, was whipped, nailed to a cross, and sealed in a guarded grave. It didn't matter—He had a destiny and an image to fulfill. In three days, that same Jesus broke all natural laws and rose from the grave, scattering the Roman guards who fell down as dead men. Then He appeared on the road to Emmaus and revealed Himself to two men who had been discussing the mysterious disappearance of the body of the "prophet" Jesus of Nazareth that day. Although they had been His followers, they didn't recognize His body until He revealed His image to them just before breaking bread at dinner. Those men let the broken, bruised, and buried body of Jesus fool them, but it didn't change His image as the risen Son of God.

Later that evening, the same Jesus walked *through a wall* into a room to confront His disciples for their fearful doubt and unbelief (see Jn. 20:19-21). They doubted His promise that He would rise again because they *saw His body* crucified on a cross. They *saw His body* lying lifeless in a tomb of stone. Now they saw that same body walk through a wall! Jesus did the impossible to tell them, *"Don't let My flesh fool you!"*

The first Adam couldn't rise from a grave, nor could he walk on water or pass through solid walls. The second Adam conformed to a different image. He said, "You can't block Me out. You can close the double bolt and arm the alarm system—but you can't stop Me!" Once He calmed them down, He said, "Let's eat." Once again, His flesh had fooled His disciples. They were thinking, "Oh, now He's just a spirit. That's how He came through the wall. He's a ghost."

Just about the time the disciples thought they had Jesus figured out, He said, "Wait a minute. It's obvious that I have to change your minds and alter the image you have of Me. I am not merely a spirit." One of the 11 didn't make it to the meeting (there's always one or two who seem to lose track of time). Thomas just couldn't accept the things the other disciples told him about that night. So eight days later, Jesus again walked right through the wall and spoke directly to Thomas the doubter. "Touch Me, Thomas. Handle My body. This is the real stuff. This isn't a prosthesis. Does a mere spirit have flesh and bone? If you don't think I'm Jesus, then put your fingers in the nail holes in My hands. Put your hand in the spear wound in My side, Thomas!"

I'm sure the disciples asked Him before He ascended, "How can You be alive? We *saw You die*!" I think we have the same problem today! We may *say* we believe in Jesus, but we *act* like He died and was buried 2,000 years ago—without the resurrection. Isn't it about time for us to change the image we have of Him? Paul declared, "But if the Spirit of Him that raised up Jesus from the dead dwell in you, He that raised up Christ from the dead shall also quicken your mortal bodies by His Spirit that dwelleth in you" (Rom. 8:11).

As we have borne or carried about the image of the earthy, so we shall also bear *the image of the heavenly*—Jesus

Christ (see 1 Cor. 15:49). You are going to have to change your image of who you want to be like. The first thing God told Israel was, "I am the Lord thy God.... Thou shalt have no other gods before Me" (Ex. 20:2-3). In modern terms, He was saying, "As a matter of fact, I don't even want you to make any images of Me—don't try to take a snapshot of Me, and don't carve or mold a gold image and compare it to Me. Don't try to figure out how I look." He doesn't want us to worry about whether He is like a black man, a white man, a Hispanic man, or a Chinese man. The last Adam is going to come, and Isaiah described His appearance as he looked by the Spirit down eons of time:

> *As many were astonied at Thee; His visage was so marred more than any man, and His form more than the sons of men* (Isaiah 52:14).

> *...He hath no form nor comeliness; and when we shall see Him, there is no beauty that we should desire Him. He is despised and rejected of men; a man of sorrows, and acquainted with grief: and we hid as it were our faces from Him; He was despised, and we esteemed Him not. Surely He hath borne our griefs, and carried our sorrows: yet we did esteem Him stricken, smitten of God, and afflicted. But He was wounded for our transgressions, He was bruised for our iniquities: the chastisement of our peace was upon Him; and with His stripes we are healed. ... He was oppressed, and He was afflicted, yet He opened not His mouth: He is brought as a lamb to the slaughter, and as a sheep before her shearers is dumb, so He openeth not*

His mouth. He was taken from prison and from judgment: and who shall declare His generation? for He was cut off out of the land of the living: for the transgression of my people was He stricken. And He made His grave with the wicked, and with the rich in His death; because He had done no violence, neither was any deceit in His mouth. Yet it pleased the Lord to bruise Him; He hath put Him to grief: when Thou shalt make His soul an offering for sin, He shall see His seed, He shall prolong His days, and the pleasure of the Lord shall prosper in His hand (Isaiah 53:2-5,7-10).

"I saw Him," Isaiah said. "He was stricken with sorrow. He was acquainted with grief. There was nothing lovely about His battered body to behold. He didn't have any form of comeliness." He said, "But I saw something else, too. He was bruised for our *iniquity*. He was wounded for our *transgressions*. The chastisement of our peace was upon Him. With His stripes...."

Yet, when Jesus physically entered our world, people could not receive Him *because they judged Him after the flesh!* "You don't look like a king, and you don't have the bank account of a king. You don't even have the gait or walk of a king. In fact, you don't have a kingdom either."

The men who held Jesus in the courtyard of the high priest blindfolded Him and began to hit Him in the face with all their strength while His hands were bound behind His back. They mocked Him and said, "Prophesy unto us, Thou Christ, Who is he that smote Thee?" (Mt. 26:68)

Pilate also questioned the validity of Christ's image in His final hours of life. "If You are really a king, then where is Your kingdom? Where are Your citizens? Tell me, are You really the king of the Jews?" Jesus was unshaken and unmoved, because His image could not be changed.

Jesus answered, My kingdom is not of this world: if My kingdom were of this world, then would My servants fight, that I should not be delivered to the Jews: but now is My kingdom not from hence. Pilate therefore said unto Him, Art thou a king then? Jesus answered, Thou sayest that I am a king. To this end was I born, and for this cause came I into the world, that I should bear witness unto the truth. Every one that is of the truth heareth My voice (John 18:36-37).

At one point, Pilate became indignant with Jesus and said, "Wait a minute! Maybe they didn't give You my resumé. Maybe You don't know who I am—I am the governor. I have power from Julius Caesar. I have the power of life and death over You!" (see Jn. 19:10) Then Jesus said, "Let Me give you My resumé—just because I'm bound doesn't change who I am. Don't let these handcuffs fool you. I know who I am, and regardless of My circumstances, it doesn't change My image of Myself!"

He told Pilate, "I wasn't going to talk, but now you have overstepped your bounds. No man takes My life, because I am Life. No matter where you cut Me, life comes out of life. You are powerless to take life from life." He said, "I am Life, and no man can take My life. But I will lay it down, and if I lay it down, I can pick up My life again!"

Pilate may have been confused, but Jesus knew who He was. He didn't need any man's confirmation or approval. He didn't need any government's permission or commission to be who He was. Jesus kept on with the plan of God. He walked according to the determinate counsel of God. He chose to die, the innocent for the guilty, so that you and I could and would *change our image!*

Look at Jesus again, but this time through the eyes of John, the exiled apostle on the isle of Patmos:

> *I was in the Spirit on the Lord's day, and heard behind me a great voice, as of a trumpet, saying, I am Alpha and Omega, the first and the last.... And in the midst of the seven candlesticks one like unto the Son of man, clothed with a garment down to the foot, and girt about the paps with a golden girdle. His head and His hairs were white like wool, as white as snow; and His eyes were as a flame of fire; and His feet like unto fine brass, as if they burned in a furnace; and His voice as the sound of many waters. And He had in His right hand seven stars: and out of His mouth went a sharp twoedged sword: and His countenance was as the sun shineth in his strength. And when I saw Him, I fell at His feet as dead. And He laid His right hand upon me, saying unto me, Fear not; I am the first and the last: I am He that liveth, and was dead; and, behold, I am alive for evermore, Amen; and have the keys of hell and of death* (Revelation 1:10-11,13-18).

John said, "He was bright as the sun. I must admit that I didn't recognize Him. I said, 'Who are You?' And then I heard that voice say, 'John, John, don't you remember Me?' I answered, '*The voice sounds familiar, but the image is different.*'" What John saw that day was the glorified person of the man, Christ Jesus. *This is the same Lord Jesus whom Pilate, Caiphas, and even His disciples neither saw nor understood. Jesus knew who He was, and He also knew that in time He would manifest Himself to all those who would believe.*

"...Because Christ also suffered for us, leaving us an example, that ye should follow His steps" (1 Pet. 2:21). The lesson that His life teaches us is to hold on to what the Father has spoken to us.

What does God say about you? What does God say about the image He has of you? I didn't ask what your circumstances are. I didn't ask you what your friends say. I asked you, "What does God say about you?" The Holy Ghost has come to change the image that you have of yourself. It doesn't matter to Him that you were abused as a child—He has healing for you. It doesn't matter that you were an orphan; you're not an orphan anymore! It even doesn't matter if you never knew your mama or daddy. It really doesn't make any difference now because you've been born again. You have a whole new family. You have a whole lifestyle, with the emphasis on life, and not death.

What does God say about you? How should you think about yourself? You don't have any business thinking of yourself as a "no-good sinner." You are out of the will of

God if you dare to think of yourself as deprived or under-privileged, as a minority, a mistake, a mishap, or illiterate. There is no way a person who has been washed in the blood of the Lamb can think of himself as a "degenerate," a "menace to society," or even a "poor pilgrim of sorrow." Stop thinking of yourself as somebody who is "never going to make it." Jesus has given you an *image transplant*. The old image of death, sin, doubt, and unbelief is out. The new image of life, holiness, hope, and faith is in! You've got a whole new image! It is time to start saying what God says about you! That is how Jesus kept His image when everyone else wanted to tear it down. Repeat what God says about you, and do it with power and authority in Jesus' name:

God says I am the salt of the earth. I am the light of the world. I am a sheep of His pasture. I am the righteousness of God in Christ. I am a child of the Most High, one of the sons and daughters of Zion, the nation of priests and kings, a member of a royal priesthood, and a holy nation!

I am part of a peculiar people. I am the redeemed of the Lord. I am the "sought out" one. I belong to God. I've been grafted into Israel, and I have royal blood running through my veins. I can leap over walls and run through troops of the enemy. Nothing is impossible because I can do all things through Christ which strengthened me. Greater is He that is in me than he that is in the world.

I am not afraid of the drug addict, the drug pusher, or gang violence. I have power to tear down strongholds and cast out devils. I have power to go through storms and tribulation. I have power to go through the attacks of backbiters and slanderers. I refuse to live under the image that the devil wants me to live under. I speak only those things that God says about me.

Paul said something about you that you need to memorize and burn into your being: "[God] hath delivered us from the power of darkness, and hath translated us into the kingdom of His dear Son" (Col. 1:13). You may still be on the planet called Earth, but God has transported, translated, transplanted, transformed, and changed your image. No matter what you thought before, since God has touched your life, *you are more than what you thought!*

Endnote

1. *Strong's*, #5481 (Greek).

Chapter 7

From Prostitutes to Evangelists

**The way you are is not
the way you're going to be.**

Simon Peter and his brother, Andrew, along with James and John, the sons of Zebedee, were rough fishermen with little or no formal education. They had followed the occupations of their fathers before them, and had no outward qualifications to be chosen to turn the world upside down. Peter especially was given to impulsive words and actions.

Another man named Simon Zelotes (or "zealous") belonged to the radical Zealot party. They actively supported the violent overthrow of their Roman captors through guerrilla warfare, and the physical punishment of "sinners" through vigilante action.

Levi (also called Matthew) was perhaps the least likely recruit in the bunch. He was a tax collector, a collaborator who took payoffs from the hated Romans in return for collecting exorbitant taxes for Rome, and cheating his own people for profit. The most likely candidate was Nathanael (also called Bartholomew), who was noted for insulting the Lord's hometown by remarking, "Can any good thing come out of Nazareth?" Jesus commended him for being so bluntly honest.

Nathanael was recruited by Philip, who is remembered for asking Jesus for "just a little more proof" of His identity after three-and-a-half years of personal, one-on-one discipleship by the Son of God. The other likely candidate was a skilled money manager and steward named Judas.

The other three disciples in the inner circle of the Twelve were Thomas (the most famous doubter in human history), James, son of Alphaeus (who may have been Levi's brother), and Thaddaeus (also called Judas, son of James). As far as we know, not one of the Twelve had any "theological training, ministerial credentials, or formal education."

We should be thankful that these men were transformed into *more than they were* when Jesus asked them to follow Him. Paul said, "And as we have borne the image of the earthy, we shall also bear the image of the heavenly" (1 Cor. 15:49). What does that mean? It means regardless of how you look, or what circumstances you are in right now, you are going to be like Jesus!

The imagination of God has said, "You are going to be like Me. I know your family doesn't see it. I know your critics don't see it. I know your enemies don't see it—but it is too late. I have already imagined it, and it shall come to pass."

Paul (whom I believe is the author of Hebrews) wrote, "Wherefore, seeing we also are compassed about with so great a cloud of witnesses, let us lay aside every weight, and the sin which doth so easily beset us, and let us run with patience the race that is set before us" (Heb. 12:1). Exactly how are we supposed to do this? I'm glad that the apostle had more to say. Paul tells us the secret to success in the next verse: "Looking unto Jesus the author and finisher of our faith; who for the joy that was set before Him endured the cross, despising the shame, and is set down at the right hand of the throne of God" (Heb. 12:2).

Can you see what motivated Jesus to put up with the contradictions and accusations of sinners against Him? It was joy. Whenever the human part of Jesus was discouraged, God the Father would show Him the image of His Church, His Bride. That image of desire empowered Him to endure the shame and torment of the cross. If it hasn't dawned on you yet, then think about it: How easy can it be to die for people who are killing you? It is difficult to give your life for somebody who has betrayed you and isn't even man enough to die with you.

What kind of Church do you think God the Father showed His Son? Did He give Him a picture of a weak, violated, sin-stained, sin-torn, jealous, backbiting, shadow of a

Church? No, Jesus died for His glorified Church, the Church that Paul saw without spot or wrinkle, without a blemish. Jesus said, "Now for that, all right, I will endure the cross and even taste death for the first time! If I go through that, then My Church will be like the image!"

I want you to know that that is what it's going to take for you to be saved and sanctified. *You are going to have to see what God sees.* Now, whenever the enemy tells you, "You can't make it," you need to turn your eyes away from the devil's conjured image of failure and look at Jesus. Then say what God says about you: "I'm going to be like Him!" That is the image we must have to endure our own "cross" each day.

The only way anyone can be saved is by changing his image into God's image—and that is impossible for man. I'm thankful that what is impossible for man is possible for God (see Mt. 19:26). It is good to know that regardless of what you face, regardless of what you are in, God is in control. The sooner we learn that lesson, then the sooner we will realize that "all things work together for good to them that love God, to them who are the called according to His purpose" (Rom. 8:28); and that "in every thing give thanks: for this is the will of God in Christ Jesus concerning [us]" (1 Thess. 5:18).

You and I need to see what God sees, but He will not show you everything that you are going to do and be all at once. You would faint! God has to show you His will for your life a little at a time. God will also remove and replace people in your life with others who will advance the cause of Christ and move you into the place that God has chosen for you. We do not have the option of choosing who will be with us.

Samuel was one of the greatest of all Old Testament prophets. Yet when God sent Samuel to anoint a king from Jesse's house, Samuel would have picked the wrong man if God hadn't stepped in! When Samuel saw tall Eliab, the first-born son, walk in, he stood up with his anointing horn in hand and said, "Wow, this is the guy! Just look at him, Lord. He even looks like a king."

God interrupted the prophet by tapping on Samuel's shoulder and saying, "Samuel, stop that stuff. Man looks at the outer appearance—you are judging by what you see. But God goes beyond the surface and checks out the heart" (see 1 Sam. 16:7). God had somebody in mind, but it sure wasn't Eliab, or the six other sons in the house. God wanted the forgotten eighth and youngest son who was still watching sheep out in the fields—the boy called David.

If we walk in the flesh, we will always be appointing and choosing people whom God has no intention of anointing. I've discovered that God has only given us sovereignty over His worship and praise on earth. We can choose not to thank or praise God, but that is about the only thing that we can do on our own. God has also declared that if we are foolish enough to hold back our praise, then He will make the rocks shout His praise. The ministry of praise is where you get involved and become active.

We have to face the fact that we can't "help God be God" because He is God by Himself. Our job is to learn how to open our mouths and thank God regardless of what we are going through. We don't limit our thanksgiving to the things God has given us or done for us—we praise and worship Him for who He is.

When Jesus set up His strike force, He seemed to grab some of the most unlikely people you could think of for a band of future "world-changers." They were nearly all misfits— just a band of degenerate folk who had a history; people who had a past they were trying to shake. Jesus chose people whom other folk didn't want to be bothered with, and He told them, "Follow Me. I will change your image. I'll change what you think about yourself and how you think in general. I will change how you walk and operate. I will make you fishers of men."

Jesus was saying, "I will change ordinary men into apostles. I will change people who are afraid of their own shadows into bold soldiers who will challenge death itself. *I will change publicans into preachers, tax collectors into worship leaders, and prostitutes into evangelists!*"

The Scriptures show that God has a habit of choosing the unlikely and unlovely as instruments of the unthinkable! He used a man and a woman past childbearing age to conceive and give birth to a nation. He used Rahab the prostitute and Ruth the foreigner to bear the Messianic seed. He used a lute-playing boy-shepherd to deliver Israel from Philistia, and He used a Christian-hating Jewish Pharisee named Saul to take the gospel to Asia. If you are not perfect, then you fit right into God's family, too. The only thing left to do is to allow God to change your image, because *image is everything*!

Image can make the difference between great success and stunning failure. The Book of Exodus features a two-man team, in which one member succeeded like few men in recorded history, and the other had a terrible failure in his life—because he had the wrong image.

Moses was chosen by God to deliver Israel from Pharaoh. They had miraculously crossed the Red Sea, and God had given Israel the Ten Commandments through Moses. The first thing God told them was, "I am the Lord thy God.... Thou shalt have no other gods before Me. Thou shalt not make unto thee any graven image..." (Ex. 20:2-4). In other words, God was saying, "Don't change My image!" God wanted the children of Israel to understand that He is a spirit. He wanted to raise up a spiritual people in His own image who would worship Him from the heart, not from obligation.

When God first called Moses to return to Egypt to deliver the Israelites, He told Moses, "I have made thee a god to Pharaoh: and Aaron thy brother shall be thy prophet" (Ex. 7:1). God was saying, "Moses, I'm going to make you like a god to Pharaoh. You are going to confront him in My place, so I don't want you to act like the frightened man who ran away in fear 40 years ago. I don't want you running from your past, afraid of what they know about you. I am changing the image you have of yourself. I know how you feel,

Moses. You think you have disqualified yourself because you murdered a man. You think it is over for you, that you can't do anything. Don't worry about it. I'm changing the image and perspective you have of yourself."

Moses tried to make excuses: "God, I stutter." God answered like He did in the garden: "Who told you that you stutter?" When Moses insisted that Aaron, his older brother, be the spokesperson, God became angry. "You are the one I've chosen. I'm making you to be like Me! Don't tell Me how to run My business. Just let Me be God. And what I say you are is what you are. If I have anointed you for a purpose, don't try to tell Me why you can't do what I've called you to do! Don't give excuses to Me about how you have disqualified yourself. Just be what I've called you to be.

"I am sending you back to the same place you ran from in fear. This time, when you walk in there, I want you to march right down Main Street—don't bother to send any letters—just walk right up to Pharaoh's house like you own the place. Remember that you represent Me.

"When you get there, say, 'Pharaoh, this is Moses. Let my people go!' Don't ask, 'Could you please, do you feel like it, if it's a holiday, can't we go?' No. Go right in there and say, 'Let them go!' When they ask you who sent you, tell them 'I AM'."

Why did the invisible God, the great I AM, send a man who ran from responsibility 40 years before? What happened to change this man who ran away a fugitive, but returned a deliverer? Moses saw something on the backside of the desert that *changed the image* he had of himself.

If you are alive, then I know you are fighting with something inside you. I know there are conflicting things in you. Like Paul, you may feel "troubled on every side; without were fightings, within were fears" (2 Cor. 7:5). The enemy does not want you to grasp who God says you are. He will stir up things on the inside that you know about yourself, just to keep you from receiving and focusing on the self-image God has for you. If you ever want to fulfill God's dream for you, then you will have to lose sight of what you "used to be."

Pick up a recent photograph of yourself. (Don't be like the preachers who send out pictures from 30 years ago, when they still had hair and were slim. If you went by their pictures, you could walk past them at the airport.) You need to get a recent photograph. The problem is that your family and friends are still looking at an "old photo" of the old you. God always begins rebuilding the image by starting with you: Who do you think you are? Once you know the answer to that question, then you can begin to show your family and friends the new "picture" and image that God has of you!

Moses believed God and obeyed. He marched up to mighty Pharaoh and said, "Thus saith the Lord God of Israel, Let My people go" (Ex. 5:1). At first it was a joke to Pharaoh, but he didn't know God had said He would make Moses as a god to him. God promised Moses that He would back up everything he said to Pharaoh. Whatever he pronounced upon them would be brought upon them. God would back up whatever came out of Moses' mouth! How would you like that? I have news for you—God has given you *the same promise!* He told the disciples (and all who would later believe on Him), "…Whatsoever ye shall bind on earth shall be bound in heaven: and whatsoever ye shall loose on earth shall be loosed in heaven" (Mt. 18:18). All you have to do is what Moses did: open your mouth.

The last thing the devil wants is for you to walk around with the image God has of you! Moses dared to trust God, and he performed ten miracles and brought the children of Israel out of Egypt carrying their captors' jewels and treasures! They marched through the Red Sea, and emerged on the other side dry and free.

Now comes the "other side of the coin." The other "half" of the team was Aaron. His life is a picture of the image held by most of the Christians in the Church today! God had warned the Israelites not to have any other gods before Him. He wanted access into their lives without interruption or distraction. He was saying then, as He says now, "I want you to see Me, because when you see Me, you get a better image of who *you* are. I don't want anything to block the vision."

God gave the Ten Commandments to the Israelites verbally through Moses in Exodus 20. He told the Israelites not to make any graven or carved images of things in the heavens, on the earth, or in the water. He told them not to bow down to them or serve them because they would change their image of God!

What did Aaron do? When God called Moses to meet Him in Mount Sinai, he was gone for 40 days and nights.

The people got restless and asked Aaron to "make them a god" to worship. Aaron forgot his image. He began to think he was supposed to match the picture the people had of him (a priest and leader who could be persuaded to do the popular thing instead of the *right thing*). He even came up with the idea for them to use their jewelry to make a golden image! Then he personally melted the jewelry, molded the image, and carved the idol himself! Then he personally built an altar for it and proclaimed a feast "to the Lord." Once a man of God loses sight of his true image, he can cause a lot of trouble quickly!

Aaron actually helped the Israelites *alter their image of who God was. He reduced the great I Am into a molten image made with man's hands* because he had forgotten who God said he was, and he had changed his image of God to accommodate his new image of himself.

Moses, who spent 40 years as an exiled fugitive and a farmer in the wilderness, stood before his people as the image of God. He stood in the likeness of the One after whom he was made. He acted, walked, and talked like he belonged to God. God wanted to let *every one of the children of Israel* know who He was by magnifying Himself *in each of them.* This is still God's plan for man.

Christians today are still playing Aaron's game every time they say one thing and do another. God is either glorified or horrified in and through us. The reason most unsaved people don't want to go to any church service or get involved with "religious people" is because of the kind of people they see calling themselves Christians.

The unsaved world is confused by the inconsistency of the Church. Jesus called Himself the "light of the world" (Jn. 8:12), but He also made it clear that we would be the light long after He returned to His Father. He said, "Ye are the light of the world. A city that is set on an hill cannot be hid" (Mt. 5:14). He also said, "Let your light so shine before men, that they may see your good works, and glorify your Father which is in heaven" (Mt. 5:16).

The unsaved world must literally visualize God's image using what they see in us! Perhaps that explains why so many people don't want anything to do with God! Light is supposed to drive out darkness and bring clarity. There is no greater reason for us, as the Church, to be careful in the way we walk, talk, and live in this world.

Our image should reflect the perfect, unchanging image of God. We should constantly be hearing people in the world say, "Here comes a saint—you know how they are. They don't like to say bad things about other people, so..." or "Here comes a saint—let's ask him what God says about this problem. He's never led me wrong yet. I think I'm going to have to become a Christian soon—I keep wanting to be just like this guy...."

The saints should be as consistent as their God. If you're having trouble, it is probably because you don't have consistency of focus. Some people think that just because they came to the church and went down to the altar once, they got it all.

"Honey, look, I know the Man."

"Oh yeah? What happened?"

"It was simple. I shook hands with the ministers. I got religion. Don't tell me I don't."

"You haven't been to church since the war."

"Well, listen, He's within my soul. Right here."

"Well, was He with you that week you were saying this one day, and doing the other thing 'with the boys' on the next day?"

"Hey, listen—I got my own thing. Me and Him done worked that all out."

We can wear each other out with empty words, excuses, and endless self-justifications. But God is not a man that He should lie (see Num. 23:19). God's Word says we are *called to something*:

For even hereunto were ye called: because Christ also suffered for us, leaving us an example, that ye should follow His steps: who did no sin, neither was guile found in His mouth: who, when He was reviled, reviled not again; when He suffered, He threatened not; but committed Himself to Him that judgeth righteously: who His own self bare our sins in His own body on the tree, that we, being dead to sins, should live unto righteousness; by whose stripes ye were healed (1 Peter 2:21-24)

What are you called to? You know you're not just coming to church because you don't have anything to do with your Sundays. There has to be a purpose behind the calling. *God called you to something.* He won't let you sleep. He won't let you "be normal." Trust me. I tried to get out of what I'm doing, but God had already called me. I didn't elect or choose myself—God did.

If God did call you, then He called you *with purpose*. The best thing to do is ask God about it. You already know there is more to it than just shaking hands with the minister, putting your name on the church roll, or serving in an auxiliary. Ask God; He will tell you. Most of the answer is already in His Word. In First Peter, He says you were called to "follow His steps."

Most people find it hard to believe that God has called us to sinlessness, but it is in God's Word. I may sound a little like an old holiness preacher, but God has called us to sinlessness! Instead of preaching, "Well, we are all going to sin sometime," we need to preach *what the Bible says*: "Who did no sin, neither was guile [trickery, deceit, or chicanery] found in His mouth" (1 Pet. 2:22).

A lot of church folk, or so-called Christians, are recognized more for their constant infighting, fretting, and loud obnoxious ways than for their holy lives and loving ways. They are like that because they are inconsistent with their vision to walk in the image of God. God gives us the remedy in the Book of Hebrews, where He says, "Wherefore seeing we also are compassed about with so great a cloud of witnesses..." (Heb. 12:1). When people who are saved act like people who are not saved, we have a problem. While we want to be a witness to the unsaved, we also need to fellowship closely with holy people who obey God. Paul was saying, "I have too many witnesses to change my theology!

Since we are all surrounded by such an overwhelming majority of godly witnesses, I would like to urge you to lay aside every weight and the sin that so easily besets you. And run with patience the race that is set before you" (see Heb. 12:1).

The next verse shows us the only way we can keep our consistency in the faith: "Looking unto Jesus the author and finisher of our faith" (Heb. 12:2a). Our focus must be on Jesus. To stay on course, we need to do what Jesus did. This can only be done on a day-by-day basis through prayer, repentance, and obedience. Like an artist painting a scene he sees every day, we need to compare our work against the flawless original:

> "Jesus wouldn't have done that—I'll take that off my image. I did that wrong yesterday—that line should change here, because Jesus is straight. Now look, that line is a little crooked. Let's move that. All right. What did I do? Oh, God, what did I do wrong? I spoke harshly? All right. Let me change that. Let me call that person and ask forgiveness, because I'm trying to be like Jesus."

This kind of lifestyle will never happen if you listen to all the religious folk around you saying, "Look, child, you don't have to be *that* saved! Now, look, there isn't any way in the world that anybody can be like Jesus!" Don't look at them—look unto Jesus, the author. He's the One who said it. He's the One who started it. He's the One who called you, not them. He's the One who saved you, not them. You were not born of corruptible seed. No man or woman can give you the thing that you have in you! It took God to place His Word inside you!

Don't get midway down the stream and start looking at people, like Aaron did. Keep your eyes on Jesus, the author and the finisher of your faith. God started it, and He's going to complete it. It is His image, His idea, and it is His joy to make you in His image. There is only one way for us to be made like Him and be conformed into His image—we must keep our eyes on Him. He wants to change us to make us like Him, but we have to look at Him and say, "Oh, I see I am a little off to the left. Let me move over to the right, Lord. I want to have Your vision, Lord. I want to look like You."

I am pleased to tell you with full authority in God's Word, backed by personal experience, that God gives us grace to take on His personality and be conformed to His image. God gives us grace to get our image right. He adjusts us here a little and there a little, day by day, as we begin to walk like Him, talk like Him, love like Him, and forgive like Him. We begin to do things that He would do—without even thinking about it! What is the purpose? God wants our lives to glorify Him. I want people to know everywhere I go that I've been with Jesus. "Say, there goes Marvin Winans. Yeah, he's been with Jesus again. Just look at his face. Look at the way he's dealing with that homeless person, that alcoholic. He took that cussin' and didn't cuss back. He didn't used to be that way, but he's been with Jesus."

John declared, "Behold, what manner of love the Father hath bestowed upon us, that we should be called the sons of God...and it doth not yet appear what we shall be..." (1 Jn. 3:1-2). We do know that when we get through working on ourselves, if we keep our focus, if we look to Jesus, then the Scriptures say, "...we shall be like Him; for we shall see Him as He is. And every man that hath this hope in Him purifieth himself, even as He is pure" (1 Jn. 3:2-3).

The call of God is a call to be like He is. To have the image of God means that we have spent time to understand what that image is, to understand who the Person of Jesus is, and then to fashion ourselves like Him. We all have a part to play in shaping who we become.

Mankind doesn't want to be responsible for their actions, but God says, "You make the choices. You can choose to handle the situation as Jesus would handle it, or you can choose to handle it your own way or the way the world would handle it." Jesus invested three-and-a-half years with His disciples so they could *imitate what He did*. The Spirit of God, the Holy Ghost, gives you the authenticity. You must cause your flesh to become subject to the Spirit so He can give you the authenticity of Christ.

You may be able to say with full assurance that you've been born again, but your flesh must be conformed into the image of Jesus for you to walk in holiness. Jesus left us an example of how to mortify or to conform the flesh to do what the God in us says to do.

The reason God doesn't just "save you and take you to Heaven right away" is because He wants to enable you, as an "earthen vessel," to walk in the midst of a crooked and perverse nation as sinless, blameless, unreprovable, and unrebukable representatives of His name and Kingdom. You are a walking "epistle" or letter to the unsaved world, openly demonstrating the power of God's grace to save, redeem, and change average people into bold leaders, publicans into preachers, tax collectors into worship leaders, and prostitutes into evangelists!

Chapter 8

What If You Were an Heir?

Can you imagine how dramatically your life would change if you discovered that you were the long-lost great-grandchild of the late John D. Rockefeller?

As an heir of this family, you would enjoy a lifestyle that enables you to shop at any store without worrying about the price tag. You would eat at the finest of restaurants. You would drive the finest cars. Overnight, all your financial worries would be erased! Not because you earned enough money, but because the patriarch of your family prepared the way.

"But my God shall supply all your need according to His riches in glory by Christ Jesus" (Phil. 4:19). The Body of Christ has suffered greatly in the area of finances simply because our image of God as it relates to money has been warped by false teaching. The Father never wanted His children to make a "god" out of riches; rather, He wanted them to know that their God is rich.

People have argued that Jesus was poor. I beg to differ with them! Jesus wore garments that were so fine, the Roman soldiers wouldn't even tear them—they actually gambled for the right to take them for themselves!

There came unto Him a woman having an alabaster box of very precious ointment, and poured it on His head, as He sat at meat. But when His disciples saw it, they had indignation, saying, To what purpose is this waste? For this ointment might have been sold for much, and given to the poor. When Jesus understood it, He said unto them, Why trouble ye the woman? for she hath wrought a good work upon me. For ye have the poor always with you; but Me ye have not always. For in that she hath poured this ointment on my body, she did it for My burial. Verily I say unto you, Wheresoever this gospel shall be preached in the whole world, there shall also this, that this woman hath done, be told for a memorial of her (Matthew 26:7-13).

Everything associated with Jesus was expensive: from the gifts the wise men brought at His birth, to the colt that He rode into Jerusalem during His triumphant entry; from the alabaster box of ointment this woman poured upon His body, to the tomb the rich man gave for His burial. The most costly gift of all was the gospel He preached, and it was this sacrificial gift that prepared the way for His children. Salvation is free, but the walk is expensive. Jesus asks for *everything*, because He gave everything!

The reason the Lord was able to maintain such a low profile is because He never worried about His needs being met. Jesus didn't worry about what He was going to eat, or where He was going to sleep. "And Jesus said unto him, Foxes have holes, and birds of the air have nests; but the Son of man hath not where to lay His head" (Lk. 9:58). He was saying, "I am not worried; God the Father is My sponsor."

When the time came to pay taxes, like many of us around the 15th of April, Peter was worried. Jesus told him, "Peter, don't be nervous. Go fishing." "What? You want me to fish—with the IRS breathing down my neck?" Jesus said, "You go ahead and fish. Now I want you to open the mouth of the first fish you catch. There will be enough money there to pay all the taxes" (see Mt. 17:24-27).

Imagine what it entails to be a son of God. You can go where you want. You can eat whatever you want. (If you make a mistake and eat something deadly, it will not hurt you. You can sanctify it by prayer.) No matter how difficult the neighborhood is, you have the power to cast out devils and take dominion over every foul spirit!

If you can just understand and believe what it means to be a son of God, then the devil will lose every fight he picks with you. I guarantee he would lose every time he brings a temptation to you, if you *recognize who you are*! Tell yourself again, "I'm a son."

The world didn't have a clue about who Jesus was. History still doesn't have a clue, because God says it cannot be found by searching. John said, "The world knoweth us not, because it knew Him not" (1 Jn. 3:1c). You can move to the Middle East and stay there for ten years on the Mount of Olives and still not find God. You can go to the Far East and join any religious group you want, but you will not find God by your human efforts. No man can come to the Father except God call or go get him (see Jn. 6:44,65, 14:6). God sets up the situations and orders the circumstances to lead us to Him. The only way for us to know Jesus is for Him to reveal Himself to us. This agrees with the words of Jesus, who said, "Blessed art thou, Simon Barjona: for flesh and blood hath not revealed it unto thee, but My Father which is in heaven" (Mt. 16:17).

Since the world cannot know the Father unless He reveals Himself, so the world cannot know who we are unless God reveals it to them. "Now when they saw the boldness of Peter and John...they took knowledge of them, that they had been with Jesus" (Acts 4:13). Stop expecting unregenerated people to understand the principles of Kingdom living—and don't be disappointed when unbelievers don't recognize and doubt your new identity.

> *Giving thanks unto the Father, which hath made us meet to be partakers of the inheritance of the saints in light* (Colossians 1:12).

> *The Spirit itself beareth witness with our spirit, that we are the children of God: and if children, then heirs; heirs of God, and joint-heirs with Christ...* (Romans 8:16-17).

Now that you know that you know you are an heir, you are entitled to the same rights and privileges that Jesus has.

What are you going to do about it? One of the most quoted verses in the Bible is the passage where Peter steps out of the boat and walks on the water to Jesus, but the Lord showed me that Peter did not walk on the water!

Now before you call me a heretic, let me complete the revelation. Jesus came to the disciples walking on water in the middle of the night, in the middle of a storm. Peter said, "Lord, if it be Thou, bid me come unto Thee on the water. And He said, Come..." (Mt. 14:28-29). Peter stepped out of the boat and walked on one thing, and one thing only, and that was the Word Jesus gave him. He was held up by the Word, and when doubt entered his heart, he began to sink.

God is calling you out of your boat of mediocrity and lack. He is calling you to a new image. He is calling you right now to a new inheritance. The time for talking is over. Now is the time for action!

God can hear you, and God can answer you. But God can't step out of the boat *for you!* When God says something—no matter how impossible it seems—you can step out on it! I don't care how many people have fallen into the water before you—if God has called you, then you can step out on His Word! It doesn't matter how many people are still hanging behind and shivering in the boat. Go ahead and tell yourself, "I'm stepping out on the Word"!

God's Word will uphold you. It will uphold you though everything else around you is falling apart! God's Word will hold you. You need to go beyond words of devotion to acts of motion! Step out in faith—trust God's Word to keep you together. When folks don't understand how you're able to stay together in the furnace of affliction, just tell them, "God's Word is holding me fast. He won't let me go down or burn up. His Word won't turn me loose because I have His Word on the inside!"

Why is God's Word so important? It is God's Word that says, proves, and authorizes you to be a *joint-heir* with Jesus! You have to have the Word of God at work in you to *change your image—*and *image is everything*! The Bible says that Jesus is literally upholding *all things "by the word of His power"*! (Heb. 1:3)! It is impossible to overestimate the importance of God's Word in our lives.

> *And when Jesus was entered into Capernaum, there came unto Him a centurion, beseeching Him, and saying, Lord, my servant lieth at home sick of the palsy, grievously tormented. And Jesus saith unto him, I will come and heal him. The centurion answered and said, Lord, I am not worthy that Thou shouldest come under my roof: but **speak the word only**, and my servant shall be healed. For I am a man under authority, having soldiers under me: and I say to this man, Go, and he goeth; and to another, Come, and he cometh; and to my servant, Do this, and he doeth it. When Jesus heard it, He marvelled, and said to them that followed, Verily I say unto you, I have not found so great faith, no, not in Israel. ... And Jesus said unto the centurion, Go thy way; and as thou hast believed, so be it done unto thee. And his servant was healed in the selfsame hour (Matthew 8:5-10,13).*

The Roman centurion told Jesus, "I'm not worthy for You to step under my roof. As a matter of fact, I know it's not even necessary for You to come to my house—it would be a wasted trip!" I'm sure the disciples must have raised their eyebrows at that comment. The Roman officer told Jesus, "Lord, You have a lot of disciples around You, but they don't know who You are. Perhaps my military experience has opened my eyes to see who You really are. I am an officer with a high rank and a lot of authority in the Roman army. My men are taught the protocol of rank, authority, and the chain of command in basic training."

The officer looked at the disciples, and then back at Jesus: "My Lord, I am a man under authority myself, and my men are under my authority. If I command my men to do something, they instantly obey because I have authority. Lord Jesus, *I know who You are.* You don't have to go to my house, because You have *all authority.* I know that if You simply speak the Word, by the time I get home, my servant will be healed."

Jesus looked at His disciples and said, "Boys, I know you've been following Me day and night, and I know that takes faith. But I have to tell you that I haven't found anybody with the kind of faith this Roman centurion has. He understands what faith is all about. If you ever learn what this Roman Gentile has learned, then you will know that all you have to do is open your mouth and speak the Word."

Jesus said, "For by thy words thou shalt be justified, and by thy words thou shalt be condemned" (Mt. 12:37). Wait a minute. Are you sure you read those words correctly? Jesus didn't say "by *My word*." He said "by *thy word*." Let me repeat this key point: Jesus said "by ***thy*** *word*" you would be justified or condemned.

The words of Ezekiel make sense now. Before God sent Ezekiel out to face all the critics, scoffers, and enemies of God's purpose for Israel, He told him:

> ...*Open thy mouth, and eat that I give thee. And when I looked, behold, an hand was sent unto me; and, lo, a roll of a book was therein; ...Moreover He said unto me, Son of man, eat that thou findest; eat this roll, and go speak unto the house of Israel. So I opened my mouth, and He caused me to eat that roll. And He said unto me, Son of man, cause thy belly to eat, and fill thy bowels with this roll that I give thee. Then did I eat it; and it was in my mouth as honey for sweetness. And He said unto me, Son of man, go, get thee unto the house of Israel, and speak with My words unto them* (Ezekiel 2:8-9; 3:1-4).

Jesus echoed the truth God gave to Moses, "Man shall not live by bread alone, but by every word that proceedeth out of the mouth of God" (Mt. 4:4b). In other words, the job of every believer is to get hold of God's Word and "eat it" or consume it! If you have God's Word down on the inside of you, then you won't need the opinions of others to confirm your supernatural inheritance in Christ. You have to walk in your inheritance to fulfill your calling in God's image and purpose. If you are brave enough to claim your inheritance in front of other people, then you have to be prepared to answer their challenges to your legal rights.

"Who says you are an heir to God's unsearchable riches? What right do you have to say you are a 'joint-heir' with Jesus, when we all know you were a sinner not long ago? Who says you can preach when you haven't had a bit of seminary training? Where do you get the right to quote the Bible like it belongs to you? Who says you can have what the Bible says?"

God said it. Jesus did it, and the Holy Ghost sealed it. Your legal papers are in the Book, the Word of God, the revealed will and testament of Jesus Christ.

Let God's Word become a lamp and a light within you. Let His Word go down into the innermost parts of your being, so it can saturate, sanctify, and inundate you! Why? When the Word of God gets down inside you, it will always *change you* and transform you. The Word will translate you from one level to another. It will renew you and reveal the new man God planted in you. The Word will make you a new creature and glorify God through you.

Jesus said, "It's not what goes into a man that defiles him. It's what comes out" (see Mt. 15:11). The Word also says, "For out of the abundance of the heart the mouth speaketh" (Mt. 12:34b). If you have "eaten" the Word, then when you get ready to speak, the only thing that should come out is the Word.

Under Levitical law, the Jews were told not to eat anything that did not "part the hoof and chew the cud" (see Lev. 11:3-8). This is a description of certain mammals, like the cow, that chews the cud. As offensive as it may sound to city folks, God is using cows to give us a very accurate picture of how His Word works in us, and how we are to "eat" His Word. The Creator made cows and certain other animals with *more than one stomach*. When a cow eats grass or grain, it goes into the first stomach and is partially digested there for a time. Later on, the cow will regurgitate the partially digested material and chew it (the cud) again before it passes on down to the other stomachs for the final digestion process. Even though a cow eats grass, it can't fully digest it just by "passing it through once." It has to chew on that food, let it rest, be partially absorbed some more, and then chew it some more before it is fully digested even deeper within its system.

What is God trying to show us? He is saying that there are a lot of things in His Word we don't understand, and won't understand immediately after we read and receive His Word. We shouldn't worry about it—God's Word is absorbed through a process, not just an act. God didn't tell you to analyze His Word; He told you to eat it. Plant it in your heart and leave it there. Later on, the Holy Spirit will bring it up again for you to chew on some more. Even later, He will bring it to your remembrance—a powerful word that can heal, deliver, and transform your life, and everything around you!

When Jeremiah was just a young boy, God planted a word in him, saying, "Son, I've sanctified you from your mother's womb. I've ordained you to be a prophet to the nations" (see Jer. 1:5). When Jeremiah said he couldn't do it because he was just a child, God told him, "Behold, I have put My words in thy mouth" (Jer. 1:9b). God was saying, "You don't understand it, Jeremiah, but it's in there."

Do you have a word from God hidden in you? It's in there. Later on after he began his prophetic ministry, Jeremiah got tired of being talked about. He was tired of being ridiculed and attacked by "his own people." Finally, he said, "Okay, that's it. I quit!" He went home and sat down, and was probably muttering some of the same things you've said from time to time: "I've had it. I'm not going to say another word. If those people are rebellious enough to buck God, then let them crash and burn. I'm not going to warn them again—they won't listen anyway!"

Did I tell you about the other "problem" with God's Word? It is flammable. While Jeremiah sat there in his gloom and doom, the Word that God planted in his belly so long ago began to regurgitate! It started coming up, and Jeremiah just couldn't stop it. He sat there as long as he could, but he finally had to get up out of his easy chair. It didn't feel so comfortable to him anymore. He felt hot, because the fires of God were burning in his belly again!

That frustrated, frazzled prophet ran down to the street and started preaching again! They said, "Hey, Jerry, we thought you had retired!" He said, "I did, but when I sat down, that Word began to come up! And when it hit me, it was just like fire in my bones!"

Can you feel the hot anointing of God rising up in your spirit right now? Say out loud to yourself, "I have the fire of

God burning on the inside. I feel a fire burning in me that just won't let me quit! It won't let me stop! I've got a fire that won't let me retire!"

God planted a word of blessing in you long ago. He has already uttered eternal words to fix your status as an heir of the Kingdom and a joint-heir with Christ Jesus. You activate that divine decree when you surrender your identity with the flesh and put on Christ instead. In that moment, you receive your legal papers of inheritance. You don't have to ask the hypothetical question, "What if I were an heir?" The legal papers have already been issued, signed by the Judge, and served by the Holy Spirit.

God is ready to give you the blessings He has *already decreed* for you, but the devil wants to stop some things in your life. He is working overtime to get you to change the image you have of yourself, and you have probably fallen for some of his tactics already. But I want you to know that it's not too late!

God has already spoken the blessing over your life. The devil will come and say, "He's not worthy of that inheritance—he's just an old has-been drunk. She was a drug addict. Why, he used to abuse his wife and was an adulterer, too! This one wasn't born with very much intelligence—how could he honor You, God? Surely You're not going to give him Your glory?!" The accuser will load you up with countless accusations, damaging comments, and negative "put downs." What does God say to all this? God says, "It is finished. My decree has already been spoken. It will not return to Me void, without completely accomplishing its purpose!"

This is the most important sentence in this entire chapter. If you let this truth sink down in your soul, you won't be moved when the devil comes around with his accusations today, or tomorrow, or next week. Here it is: "**God has blessed you, and He won't take it back!**"

Say it to yourself, and repeat it to the enemy every time he shows up: "God has blessed me, and He won't take it back! No one can make Him take it back. He's already said it, and every word that God utters comes to pass. He spoke it into existence, so I'm blessed. I am an heir!"

Chapter 9

Image Is Everything!

What exactly makes us like God? How are we able to stand in His image? Do we have His nose, His eyes, or His ears? Do we walk like He walks or smile like He smiles? What about God is like us? What makes all believers, to one degree or another, equal? What common denominator groups all of us together as men and women *created in His image*?

I hope by now you understand that when I speak of "image," I am not referring to an idolatrous icon, an empty symbol, or a false facade to fool people. I mean the *character of God*.

Are you beginning to understand why *image is everything*? God's last-day word to mankind was so important that He dispatched the same Word by whom He framed the worlds in the beginning! He sent the Heir to all things; He sent His *Express Image*: "For in Him dwelleth all the fulness of the Godhead bodily. And ye are complete in Him, which is the head of all principality and power" (Col. 2:9-10). John eloquently testifies:

> *In the beginning was the Word, and the Word was with God, and the Word was God. The same was in the beginning with God. All things were made by Him; and without Him was not any thing made that was made. In Him was life; and the life was the light of men* (John 1:1-4).

Paul, in Hebrews, goes on to tell us in chapter 11, "Now faith is the substance of things hoped for, the evidence of things not seen. ... Through faith we understand that the worlds were framed by the word of God..." (Heb. 11:1,3). This is the *same Word* by whom God spoke the earth into existence, and who upholds all things—the laws of physics, the planets, the constellations, and the molecular structures of our bodies—in their place.

The only thing the temporal realm of matter and finite existence clings to is *the Incarnate Word*. It is only the unchanging, limitless power of the Incarnate Word that keeps the sun in place and maintains the delicate balance of the dance of the planets. Should the sun be moved from her place even an infinitesimal amount in the direction of our planet, the earth would be vaporized in a fiery moment of searing destruction. If the sun should be moved in the other direction, the earth would instantly freeze into a lifeless, frigid monument of what once was, but would never be again. It is this image, it is this *Incarnate Word*, that has been burned, engraved, and stamped into our hearts.

This Express Image, this exact copy and representation of God, is the measure of all truth and wisdom. His stature is our measure of perfection, our goal in God. All the gifts Jesus gave the Church—apostles, prophets, evangelists, pastors and teachers—were given:

> *For the perfecting of the saints, for the work of the ministry, for the edifying of the body of Christ: till we all come in the unity of the faith, and of the knowledge of the Son of God, unto a perfect man, unto the **measure of the stature of the fulness of Christ*** (Ephesians 4:12-13).

God says He wants us to keep going, to keep striving, to endeavor to keep the unity of the faith. He wants to see us walk and work together, because just as God is not divided, neither is His earthly body to be divided. Division in the Church produces a divided *image* of Divinity before men. This is not the image of God in the Word, which tells us:

> *There is one body, and one Spirit, even as ye are called in one hope of your calling; one Lord, one faith, one baptism, one God and Father of all, who is above all, and through all, and in you all* (Ephesians 4:4-6).

God wants us to come into the unity of the faith and grow up into the *full stature* and image of God. Jesus, the Express Image, is the One who went down into the earth and returned again leading "captivity captive" and giving living gifts unto men! These living gifts, these men and women, are the instruments God is going to use to bring you into a greater awareness and understanding of who He is.

God has called us to work together with Him to reveal the manifold wisdom of God to the earth, and to present the true Image of Himself to this generation! The Word says God created all things by Jesus Christ:

To the intent that now unto the principalities and powers in heavenly places might be known by the church the manifold wisdom of God, according to the eternal purpose which He purposed in Christ Jesus our Lord (Ephesians 3:10-11).

God continually presents or reveals Himself to us, because at the same time a steady stream of false or foreign things try to present themselves as God, to lead us away from Him and into deception.

Pay special attention to verse 17 of Ephesians 4: "This I say therefore, and testify in the Lord, that ye henceforth walk not as other Gentiles walk, in the vanity of their mind." God says He doesn't want us to create an image of Him that is *inaccurate*. Don't distort the image!

Knowing that a man is not justified by the works of the law, but by the faith of Jesus Christ, even we have believed in Jesus Christ, that we might be justified by the faith of Christ, and not by the works of the law: for by the works of the law shall no flesh be justified. But if, while we seek to be justified by Christ, we ourselves also are found sinners, is therefore Christ the minister of sin? God forbid. For if I build again the things which I destroyed, I make myself a transgressor. For I through the law am dead to the law, that I might live unto God. I am crucified with

Christ: nevertheless I live; yet not I, but Christ liveth in me: and the life which I now live in the flesh I live by the faith of the Son of God, who loved me, and gave Himself for me. I do not frustrate the grace of God: for if righteous-ness come by the law, then Christ is dead in vain (Galatians 2:16-21).

Image (character) is everything. In the verses preceding the passage we just read, Paul had to publicly rebuke the chief apostle among the Eleven! He didn't confront Peter because of a difference over position or authority, nor because of a personality conflict, and he definitely didn't want to embarrass the apostle. Paul felt he had to confront Peter because his actions were causing the *image of God* to suffer!

Paul and Barnabas had returned to Jerusalem after spending 14 years preaching the gospel to the Gentiles with great success. They visited privately with Peter and James, and the other leaders of the church at Jerusalem, who openly recognized and confirmed the apostleship of Paul and Barnabas to the Gentiles. After the leaders gave the two men the "right hands of fellowship" and blessed their minis-try, Paul and Barnabas returned to their base in Antioch (see Gal. 2:1-9).

Meanwhile, God had shared with Peter in a vision that He was no respecter of persons, and sent him to preach in the house of a Gentile named Cornelius. Peter saw an entire Gentile family get saved and filled with the Holy Ghost there. It would seem that Peter had learned his lesson. Yet, sometimes we have deep-seated prejudices and biases that have been ingrained in us by our culture or religious background. Some things just automatically go when we are saved, but the wrong things that we hold dear have to be worked out "with fear and trembling" through God's help. Peter was headed for another "attitude adjustment."

The problem arose when Peter came to visit Paul and Barnabas in the Gentile city of Antioch. At first, Peter ate with the Gentiles like Paul and Barnabas, secure in his freedom from the law. But when James sent other Jewish church leaders to Antioch, Peter suddenly reverted back to strict Jewish legalism and quietly separated himself from the Gentile believers (the majority of the congregation at Antioch). His fear of disapproval by the other Jews even influenced Barnabas to join him. The virus of legalism and prejudice was still active in Peter's life, and it was spreading to others!

I thank God for His patience with us. I'm thankful for His ability and willingness to work with me until I choose to obey Him and do things His way. If God were like us, He would have run short on patience long ago and thrown us out—but He isn't and He didn't! He stays with us to work out the sin and to conform us to His image of perfect godly character.

God is patient enough to put up with us until He works the foolishness out of us. Peter probably felt that he had passed the prejudice test long ago, but when he was publicly pressed to choose between the vision of God and the approval of his hometown friends, he went back into the very comfort zone God had asked him to leave many years before. On the surface, Peter seemed to have all the justification he needed: after all, his *ministry was to the Jew*.

If Peter recited this argument to himself, he was partially right. It *is* important to know where God has called you. Many people fail in ministry and life because they choose to work *outside of their calling*. Because they are operating in their own strength outside of God's will and plan, they are uncomfortable and unsuccessful. This wasn't Peter's problem. This leader was in hot water because he chose to ignore a direct revelation from God out of fear of the rejection of men.

If you haven't noticed already, *God is calling us to move outside of our religious and cultural comfort zones!* We are the people created in God's image and character. God is *requiring*—let me repeat that—He is *requiring* us, as men and women created in His *character*, to love one another—even if we don't look alike, act alike, dress alike, talk alike, think alike, or shout alike!

> *That Christ may dwell in your hearts by faith; that ye, being rooted and grounded in love, may be able to comprehend with all saints what is the breadth, and length, and depth, and height; and to know the love of Christ, which passeth knowledge, that ye might be filled with all the fulness of God* (Ephesians 3:17-19).

Peter ministered mostly in Jerusalem among his own people. Because he spent most of his time in the "mother church," and probably because of his visionary and charismatic demeanor, Peter was known as the "chief apostle." He was "the man" as far as Christianity was concerned at that time, since Paul wasn't as well known among the majority of Jewish Christians.

Paul had a different background. He had been Peter's archenemy before his conversion, but after God disrupted his purpose in Damascus, saved him, and declared His purpose for Paul's life, the Pharisee cried out, "Lord, what must I do?" Paul boldly preached the gospel in Jerusalem, but God told him to get out of there. The Lord was basically saying, "It's not going to work for you, Paul. The thing that worked for Peter will not work for you! Leave Jerusalem" (see Acts 9:1-30).

God sent Paul, the highly trained rabbi, Pharisee, and member of the Sanhedrin, the Hebrew of all Hebrews, to the *Gentiles*. Sometimes God will work against your personality traits and strengths to make you what He would have you to be. You may be reading these words thinking, "Well, God created me as a *quiet* person." Hold on to your seat; God might place you center stage, with the spotlight on! One thing is for sure: God has a job for you to do.

When the pressure was on for Peter to take a controversial stand based on a direct revelation of God, he took the "easy way out." Everyone was sitting together and enjoying a meal together, Jew and Gentile alike. There was no difference between them in the Lord. They were just praising God together until some "big shots" showed up, and Peter became afraid they wouldn't approve of his "freedom" in Christ.

One of the greatest things God can do is deliver you from fear of people! David said, "The Lord is on my side; I will not fear: what can man do unto me?" (Ps. 118:6) You would be surprised to discover how many people look as if they have it together while they are really hiding desperate fears inside.

On the surface, Peter seemed to be unmatched and un-rivaled in the Church. He was held as the chief apostle of the Lamb. Yet when some other fellows showed up who seemed to be more religious and better educated, he wilted. Maybe Peter thought they were more experienced and had more knowledge in the Word. Maybe they just looked "deep," but whatever it was, they frightened Peter right out of God's will!

Paul was sitting at another table eating with Gentile be-lievers when the Jewish Christians from Jerusalem showed up. Peter didn't make a disturbance. He just got his plate, withdrew from the Gentiles, and sat over at another table with the Jews. He may have moved quietly and as unobtru-sively as possible, but it didn't matter. People were watching to see how the great apostle of Christ would react. This is the reason leaders have to be careful.

People are always watching leaders to see which way they are going and what standards they have established for their lives. People are looking for a model. Personally, I don't go to a lot of places because I know people will wonder why I am there. Leadership responsibility demands a sacrifice.

Peter didn't say anything to anybody; he just moved. As a result, everyone *who was with* Peter also moved! It got so bad that *Barnabas*, the great leader who had mentored Paul and helped evangelize the Gentiles, actually moved away from the table where Paul was sitting to join the "Jewish group."

Paul looked up and noticed that *he was the only Jew hanging out with the Gentiles*. The prejudice was noticeable. Paul thought, "I cannot afford to let this happen because *it changes and distorts the true image of the Church of the Lord Jesus!*" That is when he publicly withstood Peter to his face.

Paul said, "Peter, what are you doing?" Peter answered, "I'm just eating." Paul pressed his point, "No, what are you doing? You are to be blamed!" (see Gal. 2:11-17) The reason there is such a rift in Christianity is because of leadership. "They which lead thee cause thee to err..." (Is. 3:12b).

As a black religious leader, I am well aware of the injustice white America has inflicted on my people. I am also aware that a lot of these erroneous doctrines were birthed in religious circles. But this does not change the truth of God's Word. I am deeply concerned about a recent teaching concerning the black presence in the Bible. Although I feel it is important for blacks to know their spiritual heritage, and how many people in Scripture were of African descent, we must never lose sight of the fact that God is a Spirit, and they that worship Him must worship Him in spirit and in truth (see Jn. 4:24). It is not the seed of our forefathers that makes us Christians. It is the Spirit of God that makes us brothers and sisters. "Now if any man have not the Spirit of Christ, he is none of His" (Rom. 8:9b).

We have Spirit-filled people on one side of town preaching against Spirit-filled people on the other side of town because of leadership that is out of joint and out of line with God's will.

We have churches in the same denomination and fellowship criticizing one another. Entire churches have split over issues of baptism, the rights of women in the pulpit, tongues as evidence of Holy Spirit baptism, etc.

Someone has to have enough vision to see that this kind of bickering and division will distort the image of the Church of Jesus! Paul was saying, "Peter, if you walk away from this nation or these people, then you are also saying that *God walks away from them*, because you are His image in the earth."

Jesus told the disciples before He ascended to the Father, "Whose soever sins ye remit, they are remitted unto them; and whose soever sins ye retain, they are retained" (Jn. 20:23). Paul was saying:

> *"Peter, for you to walk away from the Gentiles **simply because they are Gentiles** means that God is prejudiced! It means that God walks away from them, too. **I cannot allow that image to exist or persist!** I cannot let people leave this meeting thinking that God is behind this act of prejudice and religious rejection—**because He is not.**"*

If the Holy Spirit desires and blesses anything, it is *truth*. The Holy Ghost brings you face-to-face with reality and forces you to be honest with yourself. If you are struggling with racism or bigotry in your heart, you don't need to act as if it does not exist. You need to ask God to remove this cancerous evil from your life, and allow you to see all mankind as your brother and your equal—especially those of the household of faith.

> *For ye are all the children of God by faith in Christ Jesus. For as many of you as have been baptized into Christ have put on Christ. There is neither Jew nor Greek, there is neither bond nor free, there is neither male nor female: for ye are all one in Christ Jesus. And if ye be Christ's, then are ye Abraham's seed, and heirs according to the promise* (Galatians 3:26-29).

This is the image of the Church of Christ Jesus; one Church, made up of all people. We may carefully screen our words to tell others only of our triumphs, but God knows our fears, and He knows what we are fighting against within ourselves. He knows our weaknesses and the secret things that we are afraid to tell others for fear they will change the opinion or image they have of us.

Peter was the chief apostle of the New Testament Church at the time, yet he was fighting a losing battle with fear! He was fighting with prejudice. Peter's experience is happening in churches across America and in the world today! The wind of the Holy Spirit is blowing, and it is blowing across racial lines, gender barriers, cultural lines, and religious affiliations. We are on the verge of the greatest outpouring of the Holy Spirit this world has ever seen! Therefore, we must face our fears and let the wind blow!

Though I might also have confidence in the flesh. If any other man thinketh that he hath whereof he might trust in the flesh, I more: circumcised the eighth day, of the stock of Israel, of the tribe of Benjamin, an Hebrew of the Hebrews; as touching the law, a Pharisee; concerning zeal, persecuting the church; touching the righteousness which is in the law, blameless. But what things were gain to me, those I counted loss for Christ. Yea doubtless, and I count all things but loss for the excellency of the knowledge of Christ Jesus my Lord: for whom I have suffered the loss of all things, and do count them but dung, that I may win Christ (Philippians 3:4-8).

Paul said, "I was blameless, but I found out something. Those things that were dear to me, I had to count them as lost. I had to lose sight of 'who I thought I was' so I could pick up 'the image of who God is'."

You need to know that the image of God is not an ethereal image of some celestial "Being" way up in the heavens—this Image, this Express Image, has nail-scarred hands and a compassion for sinners and sin-sick souls that is so strong it defied death! The God of this Image has a wound in its side, the badge of compassion on a Deliverer whose great joy is to help those who cannot help themselves. God desires to *personally* move in the lives of those who know nothing of His power. He longs to gather the ungathered, to accept the rejected, to anoint the disappointed, and to restore His glorious image to our broken visage.

I believe Paul knew that *the pain of our past is our greatest obstacle to possessing the promise of the present!* He had no problem honoring Peter as an anointed man of God, but Paul confronted Peter because he wouldn't let go of his past. I think Paul knew this lay heavy on Peter's heart.

Paul was saying, "Peter, you have to be honest with yourself. How can you stand there and make somebody abide by the law when they grew up without the law and the Jewish culture? You don't even keep it yourself, and you are a Jew! Why would you make somebody think he is justified by the works of the law when you know that if that were true, then there was no reason for Jesus to die on a cruel cross!"

Paul closes the issue in Galatians by comparing his old image of Jewish righteousness, training, and zeal against his new image in Christ. "You all remember how I was—but I want you to know *I'm not the same man.* I have changed. I have fears too, but I found out that the life I now live *I live by the power of Jesus.*"

You and I have the express image of His person living within us! The Holy Ghost lives inside me, so all I have to do is tell that old man, "Let the Lord have His way! Let the Spirit of God have His way. I can't live one day without Him. I can't live in a holy state for even one hour on my own, because the old man, that adamic nature, wants to do what is natural and sinful. I have to put that old man under subjection and let the *image of God* live in me by the power of God."

The key to allowing the image of God shine out of you is *to be crucified.* You have to allow the Spirit of God to teach you how to live and love. You don't want the world to see *you*; you want them to see the *image of the Almighty!* "Nevertheless, the foundation of God standeth sure, having this seal, The Lord knoweth them that are His. And, Let everyone that nameth the name of Christ depart from iniquity" (2 Tim. 2:19). If I'm going to claim the name, I have to depart from iniquity, or else I *distort the image.*

Chapter 10

The True Image Revealed

I t is time for the true image to be revealed. I wrote this book because *I want to change the image that the world has of the Church*! We are not a group of people who worship God blindly and ignorantly. Our meetings aren't just some kind of emotional catharsis or therapy! We don't gather together each week because we don't have *anything better to do*! We no longer behave the way we used to behave, because after the light of the Holy Spirit illuminated our minds, we got a glimpse of who Jesus really is. We saw the author and finisher of our faith, the Express Image of God, the image of our destiny.

Jesus said, "I am the way, the truth, and the life: no man cometh unto the Father, but by Me" (Jn. 14:6). Jesus did not come to show us a better way, but to tell us He *is the Way*! He did not come to espouse truth, but to reveal Himself as the Truth. He did not come to lead us to a better life; He let us know that in Him is life.

God did not "leave it to mankind's creativity" to establish an image. He thundered from Heaven in holy affirmation, "This is My beloved Son: hear Him" (Lk. 9:35).

*Watch what He does. See how He lives. Listen to what He says. Observe how He operates. Look at everything He does and is. I want you to mimic Him. This is the **Image**.*

Jesus spoke only the things He heard His Father say. He did only what He saw His Father doing. His food and drink were to do the will of His Father. As God incarnate, He had the ability to do whatever He wanted to do, but He restricted Himself to *what was already written* so He could be an *example*.

"Then said I [Jesus], Lo, I come (in the volume of the book it is written of Me,) to do Thy will, O God" (Heb. 10:7). He wanted us to have a clear, concise picture of who the Father is and how He operates.

Jesus willingly laid down His divine rights and authority. "Though He were a Son, yet learned He obedience by the things which He suffered" (Heb. 5:8). Jesus brought Himself under the subjection of God. He even subjected Himself to the earthly authority of Joseph and Mary until He came of age. He was determined to reveal the true image of God. He wanted to show us that we, too, would need to learn how to restrict ourselves to the will of God, and trust and obey Him no matter how difficult it seems.

In the face of death, Jesus chose to please His Father and cried beneath the weight of our sin and pain, "Not as I will, but Thy will be done." He left us the record and image of an obedient spirit, so we would know how to walk faithfully in the midst of a crooked and perverse nation.

In chapter 5 of the Book of Ephesians, the apostle Paul gives a wonderful discourse on the relationship of the husband and wife. In it he shows how a woman should submit to her husband in everything, and how a husband should love his wife above everything—even his own life. Yet before he concludes this teaching, he says in verse 32, "This is a great mystery: but I speak concerning Christ and the church."

The Church is the Bride of Jesus, and He is a jealous Husband. He demands total exclusivity. Christ wants His Bride to respond to Him and to stay intimate with Him and Him alone. Jesus is entitled to demand that we, His Church, give up everything, *because He gave up everything* for us! He made a public commitment in the sight of Heaven and earth. He promised that He would perform all the duties that a husband owes to his wife. He only asks that His Bride be obedient and love only Him.

> *Hear, O My people, and I will testify unto thee: O Israel, if thou wilt hearken unto Me;* **there shall no strange god be in thee;** *neither shalt thou worship any strange god* (Psalm 81:8-9).

The Book of Judges describes the strange story of Micah, a spoiled son who stole silver from his mother. (She had "wholly dedicated it" to God to "make a graven image.") Micah later confessed his sin, and this woman was so "blessed" by his brief burst of honesty that she gave the money back to him so he could give the silver to a workman to make one "molten image" and one "graven image" for their "house of gods" (see Judg. 17). But the idols weren't enough for them. They decided to "hire a man of God" so they could establish their own "personal tabernacle."

They ended up meeting a young and up-and-coming Levite from Bethlehem-judah, and hired him to be their own "family priest." Evidently these people had good intentions, but they had the wrong image—and *image is everything!* The dominant and recurring theme throughout the Book of Judges was, "In those days there was no king in Israel, but every man did that which was right in his own eyes" (Judg. 17:6).

Micah and his household were trying to concoct their own brew of holiness and religiosity. But they failed to anchor their intentions on the foundation of God's unchanging Word. They *mixed* the profane and forbidden with the sacred and holy. They had some of the important religious elements, such as the priestly ephod and teraphim. They even had a priest, but they didn't have the right image to tie it all together in God's order.

**If you don't start out right,
chances are you are not going to end up right.**

Even though Micah and his mother had good intentions and were sincere, they were sincerely wrong! Micah's mother was inundated with religiosity. She set aside a great deal of money for the sole purpose of building a temple, a replica of the ark! Micah built a house of gods, made an ephod and teraphim, and then consecrated his son. God originally gave the ephod to Moses as a garment for the priests to wear. God gave Moses the ephod to help the priests know when He was speaking. It had stones mounted in a breastplate that would light up if God was for them in a given situation.

The first part of this story illustrates the confused foundation in this family's life. What kind of God allows you to steal, and then "blesses you" for your thievery? This misguided woman and her opportunistic son were carefully crafting a "god that allowed them to feel comfortable in what they were doing." They had created a hodgepodge god in the image of their own standards and ideas of right and wrong.

The true Image declared, "Thou shalt not steal," but they created a god that blessed the son's theft. The true Image declared, "There shall no strange god be in thee; neither shalt thou worship any strange god" (Ps. 81:9). The "Micah image" permitted at least two idols, and possibly more, in a "house of gods." The true Image of God makes us uncomfortable if we steal or worship idols of any kind. Micah and his mother wanted to continue in their sin, so they altered the image of their god.

This problem in the Book of Judges has also become a problem in the modern Church. Too many "Christians" act like there is no King on the throne, and they are doing "that which is *right in their own eyes*"!

Churches around the world have a lot of images set up as objects of prayer. They may represent wonderful people who did good things worthy of remembrance, but the Bible says there is only *one Mediator* between God and men, and that is the man, Christ Jesus (see 1 Tim. 2:5). Nothing must distort that image, and no one is allowed to share His glory. He has no equal. It wasn't that the woman in Judges 17 did not have God on her agenda—she did. The problem was that she had *other gods* on her agenda, too, and God doesn't mix with any other. He is God alone.

A few years ago, I was talking to some people who were kind of "high up" in the Christian ranks, and they were well known for their many accomplishments. I asked them, "Well, what church do you go to?" They looked a little sheepish, but they said, "Well, uh, right now, we don't go anywhere." When I said, "You don't go to church?" they answered, "No, well, you know, we just have this home Bible study thing we do."

As they spoke, the words of the apostle Paul to the Hebrews rang in my ears: "Not forsaking the assembling of ourselves together, as the manner of some is; but exhorting one another: and so much the more, as ye see the day approaching" (Heb. 10:25).

And He gave some, apostles; and some, prophets; and some, evangelists; and some, pastors and teachers; for the perfecting of the saints, for the work of the ministry, for the edifying of the body of Christ (Ephesians 4:11-12).

We can never escape the need for these five ministering gifts to the Church, as they will make us ready to receive our Husband. There are some who feel their prosperity precludes them from submitting to pastoral leadership. Like Micah's mother, they would love to "legitimize" their private interpretation of Scripture, and of God and the Church, by recruiting prominent people to give vocal support for their ideas.

Paul warned us not to think of ourselves higher than we ought to think. No one is above the Word of God. When I was a young evangelist, I was ministering in North Carolina when some people came up one night and said, "Ooooh..." I looked around and said, "What?"

"Ooh, we just saw jewelry falling off of you. There were diamonds and all kinds of precious stones." When I said, "Me?" they saw their open door. One person gushed, "Yea, I saw *angels*. They were all behind you, and one was touching you on your shoulder!" I couldn't resist, so I said, "My God— you think you saw *angels*?" and I got a strong, "Uh-huh!" Then I said, "Shewe-e-e, that's something." I thought they were done, but they had one more "vision" to pull out of the hat: "Do you know what the Lord showed me?" I knew the routine, so I said, "What did the Lord tell you?" Then this person looked me in the eye and said, "The Lord told me you were going to be an apostle."

I looked at the man and said, "Me?" When he said, "Yeah," I told him, "The Bible says, 'For both He that sanctifieth and they who are sanctified are all of one: for which cause He is not ashamed to call them brethren' " (Heb. 2:11). I told him, "All I want to be is a brother." This just took all the air out of him. I felt like I had just "rained on his parade." I told him, "If I can be a brother, I can get in."

Bloodline or family heritage has always been important in Eastern cultures, and it is important in the Bible. Christ died to give us a new divine bloodline. After redemption comes purification, and this process has to do with our family upbringing.

Just as Esther had to undergo a lengthy purification and preparation process before she could marry the king (see Esther 2:3), the Bride of Christ is being purified and made spotless by the Holy Ghost in preparation for the marriage supper of the Lamb. As part of our preparation, we need to have godly training, upbringing, and mentoring in the Spirit.

If the call of the Lord is upon your life to preach, there must be a time of mentoring and training under the steady hand of a proven man or woman of God. Anointing and wisdom come through struggle. When you look at a seasoned minister, you should be able to say, "He knew something because he *came through* something!"

> *Then I came to them of the captivity at Tel-abib, that dwelt by the river of Chebar, and I sat where they sat..."* (Ezekiel 3:15).

If we are to have the compassion of Christ, the fervor and zeal of winning the lost, then we must feel what they feel. The element that made Jesus such an effective evangelist was that the people felt He understood their struggle. I heard this once, and found it to be true: "People do not care how much you know until they know how much you care."

Our churches are flooded with "fly-by-night" preachers with the preaching itch and a salesman's pitch, but who have no experience or depth. I believe there should be a trail of faithfulness, of tests, and of battles won and lost, which will allow others to go back and find out how you obtained the level of spiritual success you have today.

The generation to follow needs to be able to pinpoint with accuracy the succession of anointing. Who did you submit yourself to in your early Christian walk? What pastor, or apostle, or teacher? Have you ever served the local church as a Sunday school teacher, usher, choir member, street evangelist, or bus driver? Have you ever visited the sick in the hospitals or those in prison, or ministered to the shut-ins in their homes? Have you ever made yourself a servant, to clean the lavatories, mow the lawn, or scrub the floors? Jesus said in Luke 18:14b, "For every one that exalteth himself shall be abased; and he that humbleth himself shall be exalted."

Everyone has to sit down before God tells them to stand up. It is part of the purification process. Paul said:

And these things, brethren, I have in a figure transferred to myself and to Apollos for your sakes; that ye might learn in us not to think of men above that which is written, that no one of you be puffed up for one against another. For who maketh thee to differ from another? ***and what hast thou that thou didst not receive?*** *now if thou* *didst receive it, why dost thou glory, as if thou hadst not received it?* (1 Corinthians 4:6-7).

Paul could say this because even though he had one of the best "theological" educations man could provide, God set him aside in an Arabian desert for nearly three years while he learned how to *listen*. God gave Paul a direct revelation of the gospel and the Church in that desert that fueled his ministry for the rest of his days. There is a reason Paul left a record behind—everything that he speaks must be traceable to its Author.

Jesus said, "The doctrine I have is not Mine. It came from Him who sent Me." Anyone should be able to trace your spiritual upbringing.

He commands *all of us*, great and small, to "obey them that have the rule over you..." (Heb. 13:17). He is the one who says the younger people are to obey or serve their elders. He is the one who ordained that we learn by being taught. We can ill afford to have ministers go home and conjure and counterfeit a "more pleasing and compromising gospel" as Micah and his mother did.

Prove all things; hold fast that which is good. Abstain from all appearance of evil. And the very God of peace sanctify you wholly; and I pray God your whole spirit and soul and body be preserved blameless unto the coming of our Lord Jesus Christ. Faithful is He that calleth you, who also will do it (1 Thessalonians 5:21-24).

Image is everything, and God is out to conform His Bride to His perfect image. The Bride of Christ needs purging, and God is starting with those He has called to lead His flock. The change may be painful, especially where we have *mixed* our faith with something of our own making. We need to realize that God will not "time-share" or "sublet" His temples. He will either own, or He will disown! He will either have all or nothing at all. He has provided everything we need to live holy and godly in His sight: He gave us His Son, His Word, and the Holy Spirit who abides with us day and night.

Gold and silver are graded by levels of *purity*. The more that foreign metals are mixed with gold or silver, the lower the grade (and value). God is only interested in a *virgin* Bride, a pure Bride, a Church and a people who have eyes only for Him! You either have to believe what you believe, or stop talking. As believers in the Lord Jesus, we must believe there is *no other name*, and there is *no other image*!

Jesus did everything necessary to restore the image Adam and Eve lost in the garden. Only He went one step farther. Instead of our enjoying fellowship as the "created" walking alongside the "Creator," He created or birthed Himself within us: "...Christ *in you*, the hope of glory" (Col. 1:27).

The purpose of marriage is not to buy a new home or lower your living expenses, or to just have times of sexual pleasure. The purpose of marriage is for two to become one. Christ died that His Bride might be one in Him.

God is tired of watching His people doing what "seems right in their own eyes." He is weary of watching His Church posing as a marketplace where the sheep flock to the best orator, the best dressed personality, the best entertainer, the best vocalist, and the best educated, or the most connected minister. Jesus already showed us what He thinks about "marketplace worship." When He sees it happening, He starts gathering cords to make a whip, because He is going to "clean house." Any time the Church *mixes* the sacred with the profane, it simply becomes a religious and political entity unfit to wear a wedding dress.

My final point is this: God is too great to be bribed. He demands total commitment and honesty. When you make a real decision to live for God, you will be ridiculed because there is *zero tolerance* in your life for anything else other than Jesus. We are not allowed the luxury of placing our lives, or Mohammed, or Krishna, or Buddha, alongside Jesus. When the *image is everything*, no one else measures up. The Holy Spirit inside you will not allow you to *mix* with anything that will distort the image.

Jesus has called you and I out of darkness into His marvelous light to show forth His praise and power in the earth. Since we rest in His unchanging grace, we will resist, remove, or destroy anything that seems to veil His lovely face. We will have zero tolerance for anything or anyone who causes God's image to become obscured in our sight! That is the way it should be. I refuse to be around anything that causes the presence of God, the power of God, or the anointing of God to be diminished in my life! Why? I recognize that the only reason I am where I am is because of the anointing of God.

Sometimes we have to curtail our own activities or stop our own progress because we're not ready for certain things. Even *good things* that are out of time or out of place can diminish the image. For years, I have been urged by well-meaning people who believe in my ministry to get on television and to publish books. I had to tell them, "You know, I don't think we should be on television right now." When they asked why, I said, "I know there are some things that I need to work out. I need to straighten out some things, and establish a foundation in certain areas before we start airing our ministry across the nation."

It was only after I had peace in the Holy Ghost that I was willing to write this book or start work on other projects. Even good things can cloud your view of His image, and *image is everything*! Sometimes we can let well-meaning people push us to move too fast, before we are ready in God's timing. God wants you to stay put until He tells you to move ("Hide Me Until It's My Time"[1]). He does not want anyone to compromise integrity for fame, or even for "more effective outreach."

God doesn't bless mixture. He has called us to be a peculiar people. He says, "If you want to be Mine, then you have to come out from among them and be holy." *Image is everything.*

God is a jealous God. If you want God, then you have to come away from everything that isn't part of His image—every idle work, every form of deceit; everything and everyone who distorts the image of God in your life. If you're going to be like Him, you have to be holy, because God is holy. If you are going to be like Him, then you have to be righteous, because He is righteous. You can't move at the whims of men. You can't act according to popular demand or the latest ministry trends. You must move at the voice of God. You must move when He moves.

Sometimes God will shut up the heavens and not send any rain. Sometimes it may seem like God will not speak to you, even though you prayed all night. You have to know what you know! If He has ever spoken to you before, then hold on to what He's told you.

I give you the same confession that I give the congregation of Perfecting Church: I realize that I have no business doing what I'm doing. The man writing these words is a man who totally depends on God's anointing. I have no anointing in myself. All I know to do is to conform to the image God has given me in His Word and by His Spirit.

Like Peter and John, when they stood in front of the lame man at the temple gate called Beautiful, I close this book with a simple statement of total human lack and total divine supply: "Look on us—look at the Image. Silver and gold—academic degrees, seminary training, and formal knowledge of Greek and Hebrew—have I none; *but such as I have give I thee*: In the name of Jesus Christ of Nazareth rise up and walk—in His image!" (See Acts 3:2-6.)

Image is everything!

Endnote

1. A sermon preached by Pastor Winans. Available through Perfecting Church Media Dept., 7616 E. Nevada, Detroit, MI 48234.

Hot Books by Destiny Image